CONNECT DEEPER

5 Questions That Build More Meaningful Relationships

Richard L. Godfrey & Christine Lavulo

TABLE OF CONTENTS

INTRODUCTION 1

SECTION 1 3
    Chapter 1: We Are Designed to Connect 5
    Chapter 2: What Do We Mean By Connect? 15
    Chapter 3: The Energy Behind Connections 23
    Chapter 4: Connection Principles 33
    Chapter 5: The Beginning of Becoming a Great Connector 41

SECTION 2 53
    Chapter 6: Personal Connection is About WHAT, Not WHY 55
    Chapter 7: The BE Tools 63
    Chapter 8: Managing the "One-Sided" Connection 75

SECTION 3 85
    Chapter 9: Right, Wrong, Different 87
    Chapter 10: Living in Parallel 93
    Chapter 11: Water the Flowers 101
    Chapter 12: Conclusion 109

ABOUT THE AUTHORS 111

READY TO KEEP BUILDING DEEPER CONNECTIONS? 113

REFERENCES 115

Introduction

You've probably heard the saying, "We make plans, and the gods laugh." Well, we made plans anyway—whether there was laughter up there or not—and we made them with genuine excitement.

Both Christine and I have known Annie and Zach for years. We've admired their work, their drive, and, honestly, their ability to keep up with the whirlwind of life. Here's the twist: Christine and I had never actually met. So when Zach and Annie said yes to guiding me through the process of writing this book, I was already grateful. But then Annie went one step further. She said, "You know who would make the perfect writing partner for you? Christine." She was absolutely right.

What Annie didn't tell me—maybe because she wanted me to discover it for myself—was just how remarkable Christine is. She's not just an expert in connection; she lives it. She's prepared, passionate, and one of those people who makes you feel like you've known them forever after just one conversation. Writing about "Connecting Deeper" would have been tough if the team wasn't easy to work with. Instead, between Christine, Annie, Zach, and my wife Heather, I found myself surrounded by people who were not only ridiculously talented but also inspiring in every way. Pretty quickly, the question stopped being if we could connect deeply with each other—it became how much we could deepen that connection, and if we could capture even a fraction of that magic for you, the reader.

We think we have. This book is the result of exploring how to spark brand-new connections, nurture the ones we already cherish, gently mend those that are strained, and—in those rare, necessary moments—step away from relationships that are doing us harm.

What makes this book special isn't complicated. It's simple and approachable—you'll probably recognize yourself in more than one of these stories. It's practical—a few small, intentional shifts can change so much. And it's meant to be shared—we've already seen its message travel across the country and around the world, and the responses have been humbling and hopeful.

So thank you for being here. Really. In a world that sometimes feels like it's coming apart at the seams, we have a choice. Let's make ours to connect—deeper.

SECTION 1

Chapter 1:

We Are Designed to Connect

Christine attends a book club that meets one Thursday night a month. Attending requires a 45-minute drive, most of it in heavy traffic. She had committed to attending a meeting one May, but woke up feeling a little under the weather. To be honest, she was feeling under the weather both physically and mentally. She spent the better part of the day trying to decide how she could once again bail on the book club, even though doing a book exchange that month had been her idea. The more she thought about it, the more she knew she needed to push herself to go. She knew that if she just got there, she would be glad she went.

And she was...

As human beings, we are meant to connect. We NEED connection. And when we find ourselves connecting with people, we generally find we have more joy in our lives.

This is why we are born in families, have friends, and get to know our work colleagues. Those connections fill a space in our lives, help us feel a greater sense of purpose, and push us out of our selfish moments. Connection is essential to our survival, our development, and our sense of meaning. Connection also helps us make sense of the world around us.

As babies in our mother's womb, we already have a deep sense of connection. When we are born, our brains are wired to seek closeness. We cry to signal for comfort, and to express our needs. Any kind of eye contact, touch, or the sound of our mother's voice immediately brings a sense of calm.

When we're connected with others, our brains release chemicals like oxytocin, dopamine, and serotonin, which are the very chemicals that help regulate mood, build trust, reduce stress, and even strengthen our immune system. Therefore, connection is not just an emotional need, but a physical one as well. We thrive when we find connection.

Connection also gives us a psychological anchor. When we are in relationships that help us feel secure, we're also more emotionally resilient. When we feel fear, sadness, or uncertainty, it helps us to know that someone is WITH us to help us feel safe and capable of facing those challenges. We are not meant to carry life's weight alone. Connection helps us process, heal, and move forward.

As a matter of fact, a systematic review published in *Frontiers in Psychology* in 2023, analyzing 38 research articles published between 2000 and 2019, found that adult friendships that provide social support and companionship significantly predict well-being and can protect against mental health issues such as depression and anxiety.

Dr. Caroline Bagwell, PhD, a professor of psychology at Davidson College in North Carolina said, "In the face of life's challenges, having a close friend to turn to seems to be a buffer or protective factor against the negative outcomes we might otherwise see." (Abrams, 2023)

There have been **other** studies in child development that **show** a child's ability to thrive is directly linked to the presence of attuned, responsive relationships. Cognitive development, emotional intelligence, and even physical health improve when a child is raised in a connected, loving environment.

There's a story about a Romanian orphanage in which the children were so deprived of human connection that it made international headlines when discovered in 1989. There was a belief that the children were abandoned by their parents because of developmental or behavioral issues. However, as these kids were placed in foster care, with no expectation for substantial improvement by others, the human connection of being talked to and loved helped these children to thrive. It was the connection that made all the difference.

The fact is that we are social beings. Aristotle wrote, "Man is by nature a social animal; an individual who is unsocial naturally and not accidentally is either beneath our notice or more than human."

This can seem a little harsh, especially to someone more introverted. Some people are more naturally drawn to connecting with others, and some prefer the quiet comfort in being left alone. There was an article posted in the Canadian Medical Association Journal in 2000 entitled "Pathology in the Hundred Acre Wood: A Neurodevelopmental Perspective on A.A. Milne." From the title, you can tell the authors have an unusual lens: Winnie the Pooh. The authors noticed that the characters in the Hundred Acre Wood mirrored the many ways we, as humans, relate to the world—and to one another.

At one end of the connection spectrum is **Tigger**—hyperactive, self-confident, emotionally expressive. He's the ultimate extrovert: upbeat, resilient, always bouncing back (literally and emotionally). He's the kind of connector who bursts into a room and fills it with energy.

At the other end, we have **Piglet**. Described as timid, easily frightened, and often worried, Piglet might not strike you as the boldest friend. But when it comes to showing up, he does. He's loyal. He's present. He says "yes" to the adventure, even when it's scary.

In between are all the rest: **Owl**, full of knowledge; **Eeyore**, steady and melancholic; **Kanga**, warm and nurturing; **Roo**, playful and eager; **Christopher Robin**, gentle and grounded; and of course, **Pooh** himself—simple, kind, and open-hearted.

This charming range of personalities offers an interesting snapshot of what it means to be social beings. We're not all Tiggers, nor should we be. We don't need to be Piglet or Pooh either. The beauty of connection is that it exists across a personality spectrum—not a "best personality" formula.

Science backs this up.

As far back as the 1940s, personality researchers began identifying what would become *The Big Five* traits—five core dimensions that help explain how we engage with the world and with each other (Tupes & Christal, 1992):

- **Conscientiousness.** Are you highly organized, detail-focused, and dependable? Or do you tend toward spontaneity and flexibility? People who are high in conscientiousness often take responsibility for maintaining relationships—but may also struggle with perfectionism or control.

- **Extraversion.** Do you feel energized by social interactions or drained by them? Extroverts tend to connect easily and often, while introverts may prefer fewer, deeper connections. Neither is better—just different pathways to meaningful relationships.

- **Neuroticism.** This trait relates to emotional sensitivity. Those higher in neuroticism may experience worry or emotional ups and downs more intensely. It can make relationships feel more vulnerable—but also more emotionally rich.

- **Openness to Experience.** Are you imaginative, curious, and open to new ideas—or more traditional and grounded? Openness can shape how we approach people who are different from us, how we communicate, and how we grow in relationships.

- **Agreeableness.** This trait speaks to kindness, empathy, and cooperation. High agreeableness often means you're nurturing and considerate—but can also make it harder to set boundaries or speak up for yourself in connection with others.

These traits aren't "good" or "bad"—they're descriptions. We may display more than one trait given the situation we're in. The expression of these traits is shaped by experience, environment, and time.

Each of us falls somewhere along the spectrum of these five traits—not fixed in one box, but shaped by experience, environment, and time. And just like the characters in *Winnie the Pooh* seem to model one or more of these traits more dominantly, so it is with us, which makes our ways of connecting uniquely ours.

More recently, researchers have studied how these five traits cluster together into general personality types. According to a 2018 study published in *Nature Human Behavior*, four common personality clusters emerged: **self-centered, reserved, role model**, and (perhaps most relatable of all) **average**.

Interestingly, most people fall into that final group—**average**—which isn't as dull as it sounds. People in this category tend to score high in extraversion and neuroticism, with moderate levels of conscientiousness and agreeableness, and lower openness. In simpler terms: they're socially engaged, emotionally responsive, and generally balanced, but not extreme in any one direction.

Where we think Aristotle, Winnie the Pooh, and The Big Five converge is the reality that we ARE social beings who need to connect, but that means VERY different things to each of us. An awareness of our preferred way of connecting and a sensitivity to different approaches in others seem to be the fundamental takeaways. In other words, we all want to connect—just not in the same way every time.

Most of us have been to a lot of wedding receptions, family reunions, high school reunions, or other major social events. You have to decide what to do every time you attend one of these. Do you seek out people you know or go meet new ones? Do you hang back and wait to be invited to interact or jump right in—even if you don't know anyone at the table? Do you spend as much time listening and considering other points of view in the conversation or bear down and defend your own ideas at all costs? Do you feel nervous or comfortable right away? Do you take time to settle in?

How we approach these social events doesn't define our desire to connect with others. What it does is give a little insight into how each of us likes to approach connections. And it allows us to connect differently depending on how we are feeling in the moment.

When you consider all the research, you see evidence that we do have a human need to be connected, but that can look different for everyone. Connection does not have to be spending time with people all the time. We can have a desire to be alone, or to interact very minimally in certain situations. In fact, we live in a world today where we've become much more interested in practices like meditation, mindfulness, or just "being still." Connecting to our higher selves prepares us to better connect with others.

Richard is a VERY early morning person. One of the best things about being that kind of person is that no one is up that early most days, which gives him the time to meditate, pray, read, and invest time in himself without feeling he's taking that time away from others. He needs that "alone" time. It helps him organize his thoughts, explore new ideas, and prepare for the day ahead. It's almost like connecting with self is a prerequisite in his life for being better at connecting with OTHERS as the day unfolds.

Likewise, there have been times when Christine has made it a priority in her life to wake up early and have Quiet Time—also starting her day with prayer, meditation, reading, and exercise. When practicing this, it made a huge difference on how her day went. Connecting with herself and a higher power also helped her better connect with others.

Being alone (by choice) is definitely not the same as being lonely. Whereas being alone is a form of connection, being lonely feeds into being disconnected. Once again, quoting from an online AI summary of research on loneliness:

Research indicates that social isolation significantly impacts the "social brain network," causing structural and functional changes in brain regions… leading to reduced responsiveness to positive social interactions, heightened sensitivity to negative social cues, and potential cognitive decline, particularly in areas related to memory and decision-making; **essentially, the brain appears to become less engaged with social stimuli when experiencing isolation.**

The social brain network is a concept (Johnson et al., 2005): "One of the most important functions of the brain is to identify and make sense of the behavior of other humans. As adults, we have regions of the brain specialized for processing and integrating sensory information about the appearance, behavior, and intentions of other humans."

In other words, as we move from childhood into adulthood, our brains create connections to assist in communicating across various areas in the brain. These connections make us better connectors. Creating, improving, and repairing these "connections" is the job of a lifetime.

We start developing these connections at a very early age: interacting with siblings and playmates, playing with toys and building make believe worlds, watching adults and copying adult actions. We shift our focus from siblings and toys to a larger group of family, friends, spouses and partners, jobs, activities, and hobbies as we age. The process remains fundamentally the same. What has changed with today's technology is how much easier it is to connect and build relationships with people all over the world. It's also easier to disconnect from others and get drawn into mindless scrolling and endless searching, replacing connection building with entertainment. Mary E. Andrews points out that, "Neuroscience highlights some of the ways that social media use might engage brain systems that support humans' motivation and ability to connect with others, hence contributing to some of our most important emotional experiences."

Our relationships give depth and meaning to life. Think about the moments that have mattered the most to you. The shared joy, quiet comfort, the tears, laughter and breakthroughs—they're all rooted in connection. When we give and receive love and encouragement, and are present with others, we discover not just who they are but who we are. We are not designed to be independent, but rather interdependent. Connection isn't just about how we survive, but how we come alive!

Take a moment to reflect on the connections in your life:

Have you ever felt a surge of joy after a heartfelt conversation with a friend?

Have you ever found comfort in a simple smile from a stranger on a rough day?

Have you ever noticed how sharing a laugh can instantly lift your mood?

Have you felt the sense of acceptance as you had an intimate conversation with a partner in which you felt heard and understood?

Connections are so powerful that they can:

- Reduce feelings of isolation and loneliness.

- Buffer stress by managing the negative impacts of a situation or experience.

- Assist and improve our coping mechanisms.

- Encourage healthy behaviors including exercise and healthy eating.

- Speed up recovery from trauma.

- Foster resilience.

Sometimes those connections become lost, strained, or damaged. This can happen for a variety of reasons. Regardless of the cause, if we're willing, it's never too late to rebuild those connections and create new ones. As you move forward through this book, remember that baby steps can fix broken bonds or improve difficult relationships. The important thing is to take that first step. This is where it starts. Choose one person, one moment, and watch things start to change and turn around, and those connections get stronger.

Chapter 1 Reflection Questions

When was the last time you pushed through resistance and showed up for a connection?

What do you do in your daily life to reconnect with yourself? How does that daily activity affect your relationships? Does it help or hinder a relationship?

Is there a relationship in your life that feels distant? What small step could you take to move closer?

Chapter 1 Challenge

We are wired for connection—but in a fast-moving world, it's easy to miss the moments that bring us closer to others.

For this chapter, your challenge is to become more *aware* of the small, everyday connectors all around you—and to lean into them with intention.

Step 1: Slow Down and Observe

Look for moments when connection is possible:

- A smile from a stranger
- A coworker asking how you're doing
- A family member sharing a small detail of their day

Jot down what you notice.

Step 2: Choose One Small Act of Connection Each Day

Examples:

- Send a quick text to someone you haven't talked to in a while.
- Make eye contact and offer a genuine "How are you?"
- Be fully present during a conversation—no phone, no multitasking.

What small connection did you choose today?

Step 3: Reflect on the Experience

At the end of the week, ask yourself:

- How did it feel to be more intentional about connecting?
- What surprised you?
- Who felt closer because of your effort?

Final thoughts:

Chapter 2:
What Do We Mean By Connect?

Let's take a moment to talk about what we mean in this book when we talk about connection. Most of us have people in our lives we want or need to connect with. Spouses or partners, children, parents, and siblings are common ones. Of course we want to connect with friends. Sometimes we may need to build a connection with people we don't necessarily choose, such as coworkers, bosses, even family members.

*To **be connected** means to form a bond or mutual understanding that goes beyond surface-level interaction.* That deep connection is nourished when you share a sense of being seen, heard, and valued by each other.

At its core, connection involves:

- **Emotional resonance**—feeling understood or relating to each other's emotions and experiences.

- **Mutual presence**—both people are genuinely attentive and engaged in the moment.

- **Trust and openness**—there's a sense of safety that allows one to be authentic without fear of judgment.

- **Shared meaning**—you find common ground, values, or experiences that create a sense of belonging or partnership.

Connection can happen through conversation, shared experiences, simple moments of eye contact, or even shared silence where everyone feels in sync. True connection leaves people feeling less alone and more *known*—not just for what they do, but for who they are.

In today's world where technology has changed much of the way we interact with each other, we have found that there is more divisiveness and contention and less compassion and understanding.

We propose that connecting takes place when we find "WITH" spaces—spaces where we are WITH that person (finding similarities) rather than AGAINST (focusing on differences). We all have something in common with everyone—even if just that we are human. From there, we can find other commonalities. In those commonalities, we can find additional WITH spaces. Rather than focus on our differences, we focus on our similarities. And then we can find a way to be WITH that person.

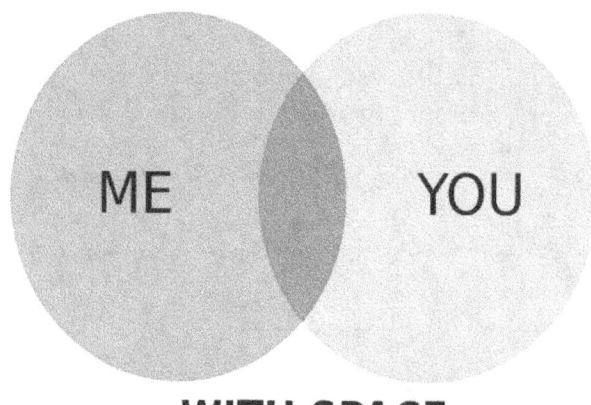

WITH SPACE

It's easy to build WITH spaces with the people that you have a lot in common with. However, it can be very challenging to find those WITH spaces when you have very little in common.

Let's look at an example of someone who may at first blush be more difficult to connect with. Through some simple steps we will show you how you can find a WITH space…

Christine has five sons. One of them is very strong in his political convictions, but those political convictions differ from hers. There have been a lot of contentious conversations when specific political topics come up. For years, she would fight and argue with him, and stick to her opinions, trying to help him see her point of view, while he pushed his own beliefs and wanted her to see his point of view. It became frustrating, tiresome, and caused a lot of disconnect between two people who love each other.

Finally, Christine decided to look for areas where their beliefs were more aligned. She stopped engaging in the conversations that caused more disconnect. She chose to seek first to understand, and she chose to listen, and she worked to direct the conversation back to those WITH spaces where they could connect.

Think of someone that you might have little in common with, but you either want or have to connect with. Now look at the list and determine what you are WITH them on and what you are against them on.

With Them	Against Them

Now take a little longer and think a little harder… is there anything else you can find that you are WITH them on?

Often, the differences have a lot to do with upbringing, circumstances, experiences, and maybe even genetics. Being connected with people that have a more diverse background can be a benefit because those differences tend to fill in for our deficiencies.

There's a story of a husband who would ask his wife for orange juice every time he got sick. And every time he asked for it, she would bring him a small juice glass with his juice. He would continue to ask for refill after refill. This caused her to feel aggravated with him, and so she finally asked him, "What is the deal with all the orange juice?" To which he responded, "As a little kid, my mom would bring me a large glass of orange juice every time I got sick, so that the vitamin C would help me get well." He associated the large glass of OJ as both wellness and healing and also LOVE. Not understanding his needs and because of her upbringing, she would only give him small glasses of juice. Why only a small glass of juice? She was raised in a home with very little money where juice was a luxury. As a child she was taught to ration out the small amounts of juice that they did have.

Their difference in "seeing" things was leading to a disconnect until they chose to see things through a different lens—what we call a "Belief Window."

We all have a "Belief Window." It sits in front of our faces and it's invisible. Imagine that a wire comes from the back of your head across the top and hooks into that window. Every time you move your head, the window moves with you. You look out into the world through this window; you accept information from the world through this window. On this window you have placed thousands of beliefs that you have accepted as correct and true (often without questioning or testing them for accuracy).

This "window" is covered with beliefs we've picked up over time: ideas about ourselves, others, and how life works. In the diagram above you can see that they're "written" on the window—and there are thousands of them, not just beliefs about Dobermans. These beliefs affect our decisions, shape our behaviors, and ultimately influence our outcomes. Some beliefs are empowering, others are limiting. Some are accurate and useful, some are profoundly false and damaging. The challenge lies in the fact that we rarely stop to question them, we just act on them as if they're facts.

If the results in your life aren't what you want—strained relationships, repeating patterns, burnout—it's worth checking what's written on your Belief Window. Are you living by the idea that you must earn love by over-giving? That conflict means failure? That vulnerability is weakness?

When you identify and challenge those old beliefs, you open the window to clearer vision, more authentic choices, and stronger connections. The truth is, when you examine and challenge your beliefs about connection and relationships things can start to change–for the better.

Let's look at the belief/behavior/results connection with a simple example: beliefs about Dobermans. At one time it may have been common for some of us to believe that Dobermans were vicious and aggressive dogs (and some are, but many aren't). As we become more familiar with these beautiful animals, we may challenge our initial belief and substitute a more generous, though cautious, belief that reads "Dobermans are all different. I shouldn't judge them in advance of engaging with them."). The belief that ALL Dobermans are dangerous has changed for many people. We know people today who feel safe around Dobermans and see them as trusted companions.

Because of what you've written on your belief window, you may be making judgments about people or situations based on those untested beliefs rather than using the actual information you're experiencing through that connection. In order to improve your connections, you may need to rewrite what's on your belief window.

When thinking about your beliefs, think about what will meet your needs over time. Often, we look only for ways to meet our needs in the moment rather than recognizing that although we can get our Amazon order sometime the same day, life isn't really about instant gratification. Many of the best things in life (such as great relationships) take time.

In order to see the difference between what will meet our needs in the moment, and what will meet their needs over time, we want to first become aware of what is on our belief windows.

What stories have you written on your window? What experiences have you had that have created those beliefs?

We have thousands and thousands of beliefs about everything, including our relationships and connections. Sometimes those beliefs are false and interfere with healthy relationships; sometimes they are accurate and help us make our relationships safe, healthy, and mutually beneficial. In any relationship, looking for "WITH spaces" and being open to challenging and changing our beliefs can be the critical opening to better connections in all areas of our life.

Chapter 2 Reflection Questions

What are some core beliefs I hold that shape how I view other people?

How might my upbringing or past experiences affect my ability to connect with others?

Have I ever misunderstood someone because I assumed their beliefs were the same as mine? What happened?

Chapter 2 Challenge

Think of one person you find difficult to connect with.

This could be a colleague, a family member, or someone in your community. Maybe you've had past disagreements or just don't "click."

Step 1: Write down your beliefs about this person.

What assumptions have you made about them? What story plays in your mind when you think about interacting with them?

Step 2: Look for a WITH space.

Now, shift your focus. What do you have in common? Have you shared any similar experiences, values, or emotions—even if your opinions differ? Write down at least **two areas of possible connection.**

Step 3: Take a small action this week.

Reach out with curiosity rather than correction. Ask a question. Offer a compliment. Share a moment of real presence. Your goal isn't to fix anything—it's simply to connect.

Remember: Connection isn't about changing others. It's about changing the space between you.

Chapter 3:

The Energy Behind Connections

Saturdays are supposed to be for relaxing—maybe sleeping in, scrolling through social media, or enjoying a backyard barbecue. That's the theory.

This particular Saturday included a non-stop to-do list. Richard got up early to clear emails, send thank-you notes, and catch up on reading. Then, as soon as the stores opened, he was out the door—picking up supplies at Home Depot, grabbing groceries, dropping off Amazon returns, and finally, stopping for gas.

By mid-morning, he was exhausted. And just as he was running low on energy, his car was too—the low fuel light popped on, seemingly mocking him. Getting gas was supposed to be the *last* thing on his list, something he'd do on the way home. But there he was, forced to stop.

Richard's favorite place to fill his gas tank is Harmon's Grocery Store and his location has a full-service attendant on duty. As he pulled into the station, an attendant approached with a cleaning wipe and asked, "Would you like help pumping your gas?"

Richard's immediate gut reaction? *What? Do I look like I can't pump my own gas?* His irritation flared, even though the poor guy was just doing his job. Richard was already running on fumes, and now even a simple offer of help felt like an attack.

At that moment he had a revelation: **He wasn't just low on gas—he was low on energy.**

The invisible fuel gauge

Cars come with a fuel gauge to let us know when it's time to refuel. Unfortunately, people don't. But that doesn't mean we don't have warning signs. The challenge is, we often miss them—until it's too late.

For most of us, that gauge measures persistent stress. It doesn't always show up as a glaring red light; it often starts small—irritability, sleepless nights, or a steady rise in blood pressure. But when we don't pay attention, those signs can build into something far more draining.

Think about the last time you had to wait forever in line at the store. That sense of impatience and frustration? Energy drain.

Or how about when you're trying to make a purchase, and the cashier is distracted, leaving you feeling like your time isn't valued? Another drain.

Ever found yourself endlessly scrolling through social media, hoping for a little positivity, only to end up feeling more disconnected than before? Yep, that's a drain too.

And then there's the overwhelming pressure of an ever-growing to-do list. You know the one—the list that seems to stretch into eternity, leaving you exhausted just by looking at it? A massive drain.

These are the little moments that chip away at our energy, and unless we learn to recognize them, they can quietly steal the fuel we need to feel our best.

By the time Richard got home, he was wiped out. Then the second he walked through the door, his wife said, "Jonathan called. Call him back."

Great. Now what? he thought.

Richard called him, and Jonathan immediately said, "FaceTime me," and hung up.

Feeling slightly exasperated at this point, Richard dutifully clicked on the Facetime icon and selected Jonathan's name and was met by his two-year-old granddaughter, Esme, staring straight into the camera.

"Hi, hi, hi!" she squealed. "High five!" She pressed her little palm up to the screen, waiting for him to do the same.

And just like that, Richard was recharged.

The exhaustion, frustration, and stress melted away. He wasn't running on empty anymore—he was instantly filled with energy. More than that, he was filled with joy!

Energy Drains vs. Energy Boosts

If you've ever driven a big diesel truck, or know something about big diesel trucks, you might know about commercial gas pumps. They pump fuel at hyper speed, filling up the tank in seconds. That's exactly how Esme's high five felt—a *fast fuel-up* of the best kind.

It made us wonder: *Why did his energy shift so fast?*

We did a little research and came up with the following. It represents input from quantum science and a branch of philosophy known as quantum mysticism. The quote brings together three basic ideas: we are beings of energy, that energy is part of everything we do, and the energy can be affected or changed by how it is seen as much as by how it is experienced.

"Quantum physics and human energy philosophies share a belief that everything is made of energy, and the observer can influence the outcome."

Translation? **Our energy isn't just about what happens to us, it's about how we perceive it.**

- What we perceive as negative interactions *drain* us.
- What we perceive as positive connections *fill* us up.

That gas station attendant wasn't *actually* insulting Richard—maybe Richard *interpreted* it that way because he was running low on his own energy/fuel. And maybe, just maybe, Richard had more control over his energy levels than he thought.

Managing your energy like a pro

Think about your average day. Some things will always drain your energy—traffic, frustrating coworkers, kids who *suddenly* remember their science project is due tomorrow. But other things can fill you up—laughing with a friend, a hug from your child, a random act of kindness.

Moving forward, how can you manage your energy better?

1. **Recognize the drains.** What people, situations, or habits leave you feeling exhausted?

2. **Find the fast fill-ups.** What instantly boosts your mood and energy?

3. **Shift your perspective.** Can you reframe a frustrating moment to make it feel less draining?

Connections are fuel

Here's the biggest takeaway: **Much of our energy is tied to our connections.**

- Some interactions drain you.
- Others fill you up.
- And you have more control over this than you realize.

Life isn't about eliminating every energy drain (because let's be real, that's impossible). But if we can create more moments of *connection*, we can keep our tank full enough to handle whatever comes our way.

So, the next time you're running on empty—physically or emotionally—find your fuel. It might be a FaceTime call, a deep breath, a walk outdoors, or just choosing to see things differently.

Because the more you fill up, the more you have to give. And that's what really keeps you going.

Lopsided Connections – Where I do most of the "filling" and they do most of the "draining"?

Imagine you're at the grocery store, juggling a baby in a carrier, a toddler pulling at your hand, and another child squirming in the cart. You're exhausted, trying to keep everything together. An older woman walks by and says, "It'll all be worth it one day," then keeps going. No offer to help, just a platitude.

This scenario highlights the emotional labor many women carry—not just in parenting but in all relationships. Women are often expected to manage everything and still smile through it. Don't get us wrong—men can find themselves in this situation as well; however, it seems to be more common with women.

In our personal relationships, we may sometimes find ourselves giving more than we receive. While it's natural to invest in our children, it can feel draining when adult partners or friends don't reciprocate our efforts. This imbalance can lead to resentment and burnout.

Roy F. Baumeister, writing in the Encyclopedia of Social Psychology talks about social compensation—where one person overextends to make up for another's lack of effort. While overextending might keep things afloat temporarily, it's unsustainable and often leads to dissatisfaction.

Similarly, the "helper therapy principle" suggests that helping others can boost our self-esteem. However, if our help isn't acknowledged or reciprocated, it can lead to emotional fatigue. It's important that we gauge our responses when we are asked for help for this very reason. When the request is something you know is needed (such as a request to babysit a sick grandchild because your son/daughter can't miss another day of work and you have more flexibility), a reframe might be in order to help you serve without becoming resentful.

How do you reframe? You change the way you view the situation (you adjust your Belief Window). Rather than feeling like you are always the "go-to" person, look for the joy that the service might bring to you.

Consider how these moments of opportunity might seem like they will drain you but end up filling your tank instead.

With that said, healthy relationships are built on mutual support and effort. That doesn't mean keeping score, but if you find yourself constantly giving without receiving anything at all in return, it's essential to set boundaries and communicate your needs. Remember, your well-being is just as important as the relationship itself, but YOU have to make those needs known.

Fostering mutual effort

Here are some steps to foster mutual effort in relationships—especially when you're feeling the imbalance of doing more than your share:

- Communicate openly: Use "I" statements to express your feelings without blame. For example, instead of saying, "You never help," try: *"I feel overwhelmed when I handle everything alone."* This keeps the conversation honest and productive, not combative.

- Set clear boundaries: Define what you're comfortable with and what you expect in return. Boundaries help maintain balance and prevent resentment. Christine was once taught to ask these three questions: *"What am I willing to do? What am I NOT willing to do? And what do I think is best for everyone involved?"* This framework helps to create boundaries that are not only logical—but ones that we can stick to.

- Encourage shared responsibility: Invite the other person to step in. This doesn't have to be heavy or confrontational. It can be as simple as asking them to plan the next outing, handle a small task, or weigh in on a decision. Mutual effort grows in spaces where initiative is shared.

- Evaluate the relationship: Step back and consider whether the relationship meets your emotional needs. If the imbalance continues despite your efforts, it may be time to reevaluate its dynamics. That doesn't necessarily mean cutting ties with a parent or divorcing a spouse—but it might mean seeking tools like counseling, mediation, or coaching to restore balance and rediscover connection.

The Energy of Connection

When we start paying attention to how our energy rises and falls throughout the day, we begin to see a pattern: our connections matter. And not just the monumental ones—but the quiet, seemingly ordinary moments, too. The friend who sends a kind message. The partner who meets you halfway. The child who pulls you into joy with a spontaneous "high five." The stranger who makes eye contact.

These interactions—small as they may seem—reveal what energizes us and what depletes us. They help us see where we need to set firmer boundaries or shift our perspective. Life will always bring responsibilities and relational tensions, but connection—when mutual and healthy—is what restores us. It's what fills us back up when we've given so much.

As you go about your day, begin to notice:

Is this moment draining me, or filling me?

Is this connection one I can nurture—or one I need to reframe or gently release?

Because the truth is this: You can't give from an empty tank. And you don't need to run on fumes to prove your worth.

Refueling isn't a luxury. It's a rhythm. And the more we learn to recognize what truly fuels us, the more alive, connected, and grounded we become.

Chapter 3 Reflection Questions

What situations or relationships consistently drain your energy—and what signs do you notice when you're running low?

What people, moments, or practices help refuel you the fastest? How can you create more of those in your daily life?

Are you giving from a full tank or from fumes? What boundaries or rhythms could help you protect your energy and connection moving forward?

Chapter 3 Challenge

For the next 5 days, pay close attention to how your connections affect your energy. Create two simple lists each day:

1. People/Interactions That Energized Me

2. People/Interactions That Drained Me

Then, ask yourself:

- What specifically made that interaction energizing or draining?

- Was it the person, the topic, the tone, or the setting?

- What boundaries or shifts might help protect my energy going forward?

Bonus Step:

Choose **one connection** that consistently drains your energy and experiment with one small shift—this could be setting a boundary, limiting the time spent, changing the topic, or expressing your needs. At the end of the week, reflect on how this impacted your energy.

Chapter 4:
Connection Principles

While we were writing this book, we both realized that when our kids were young, we used to love when the new Disney movies would come out. We had similar stories of watching them with our children over and over again. We also discovered that we both loved the movie, Pocahontas. In this Disney version, Pocahontas attempts to convince John Smith that using nature and its gifts carefully is vital to survival because everything in nature, including humans, are connected.

It's hard to get the song out of your head…

"The rainstorm and the river are my brothers. The heron and the otter are my friends.

And we are all connected to each other, in a circle, in a hoop that never ends…"

Richard and his wife, Heather, recently had the opportunity to do an expedition cruise in the Galapagos Islands. This is a place where you can really see how connected everything is. This is the place made famous by Charles Darwin's observations as he traveled as part of the crew of The Beagle. His observations on the connections between animals, plants, birds, and fishes gave rise to his Theory of Evolution–which has disconnected people ever since.

Darwin's observations on connectedness in nature, as he observed in the Galapagos Islands, illustrate some important principles of connection in our lives, just as they do in the lives of the organisms he observed.

We have carefully checked with experts to make sure that the following principles represent accurate reflections of the things Darwin observed.

Principle One—Connection helps us thrive in harsh environments

One of Darwin's most famous observations is adaptation in the shape and function of the beaks of finches on the islands of Galapagos. He noticed that finches that lived higher up in the forest canopy who got their food from nuts had developed short, sharp beaks perfectly adapted to cracking open the nuts and seeds they used as food.

On the other hand, finches that lived on the very rocky shore of the islands and looked for insects and other small animals who lived in the cracks and crevices in those rocks developed beaks that were long and narrow enough to reach deep into the rocky spaces and get to what they wanted to eat.

Just as the finches find ways to connect to the realities of their environment to get food, we adapt to situations we find ourselves in, often through connection, to survive and hopefully thrive. When Richard has lost jobs in his life, he and his wife have worked to make their savings last by limiting their spending as much as possible and by picking up extra work when possible. There were times when Richard and Heather were young parents—when both of them held down multiple jobs–cleaning houses, making and delivering pizza, working a customer service desk, working in an automotive plant (and sometimes all at the same time), while raising two children–just to get by until things got better, until the "environment" was less harsh.

It was their connection to each other, to the commitment they made to raising and caring for their children and, fortunately, the availability of different sources of work that allowed them to find their way through those harsh "environments."

Likewise, when Christine was a young, single mom, she did whatever work was necessary. Getting married provided two sources of income, but sometimes the cost of childcare would make her feel that it made more sense to stop working and stay home with their children. When times got tight, she would find whatever job worked best for her family.

There were often tough decisions they had to make while raising their family and going through the various stages of life.

We've both found, and so will you, that it was the connection to each other, to the commitment we made to raise and care for our children that allowed us to find our way through those harsh environments.

Principle Two—Connection helps us develop traits that enhance our lives

Camouflage is a principle of adaptation that makes it possible for animals that lack the size or the strength to defend themselves to survive. For instance, baby birds, mottled brown in color and nestled deep into a nest made of bits and pieces from the tree they're lodged in are very hard to see, from above and below, where predators are looking for easy prey.

Vibrant displays, the opposite of camouflage are also traits that assist in survival and making that organism's life "better." In the oceans around the Galapagos, brightly colored fish signal that they're not "good to eat" so that larger predators leave them alone. On land, brightly colored and very poisonous caterpillars signal to birds that "choosing me for lunch will not go well for you."

It's fascinating to watch babies and children learn the art of both camouflage and "vibrant display," a practice that, if it persists in life, can be very valuable once they are adults living in the real world. The art of "picking your battles" is both a camouflage and a vibrant display activity. Wisdom is rooted in knowing when to lie low and keep your opinions to yourself, and when to stand up (and stand out) for something that matters to you or others.

In a later chapter we'll explore a very simple and powerful tool for deciding when, in a connection scenario, you choose camouflage and when you go for vibrant display (it's called the Two Question Model).

Principle Three—Connection helps us reproduce successfully

Well, that's a catchy header if you've ever read one, isn't it? But in reality, it is true in every sense of the phrase. We're referring to Darwin again. He's talking about reproductive advantage in the literal sense—connecting with your environment in ways that allow many of your offspring to survive and to go on to reproduce future generations. Although wanting our children to survive and thrive is definitely important to all of us, we're going to explore this idea in a slightly less literal way.

We all have values, beliefs, skills, and talents that are useful to us and to those around us.

Have you ever been to a party or activity where you went or met up with someone you knew? And while at the party you were introduced to someone they knew? You likely discussed some things you had in common and by the end of the party, you had not only strengthened current connections but connected to new and more diverse people. This is social reproduction; connections grow when we make an effort to connect.

This phenomenon is not limited to physical interaction. This is the 21st century, when we can socially reproduce and extend our connections through social media and other online resources.

Principle Four—Connection helps us use energy efficiently

If you've ever tried to convince the family dog to "play ball" on a hot summer's afternoon, you've experienced the energy efficiency principle in action. That principle was in full effect when Richard and Heather moved into their new house. They moved into a neighborhood where they knew no one—they had no connections. On the Saturday morning the sod was delivered, Richard fully expected to lay all the grass on his own. He was younger and reasonably fit, had laid sod as a part-time job as a teenager and was sure he could get the job done. Heather, who would usually be right there with him, was recovering from surgery and unable to help.

Richard wasn't totally foolish. Living in a high desert whereby late afternoon the summer temperature is well over 100 degrees Fahrenheit, he started early. At first, things went reasonably well. Heather would look down from her bedroom window to make sure he was okay and would, in considerable pain and discomfort, bring him lots to drink. However, about five hours in, he couldn't go any further. All the energy he had was completely gone. He barely had enough energy to get himself into the house before collapsing.

And that is when Heather, who also knew no one in the neighborhood, just reached out to friends who might have friends in their new neighborhood—and some of them did. Within a few hours, complete strangers arrived and, in no time at all, the sod was laid, new connections were made, and Richard learned an important lesson about using energy efficiently. The best way to use limited stores of energy is to build connections where you can appropriately leverage the help you need, rather than trying to go it alone.

Principle Five—Connections can be close or far

In this day and age of technology, the most connected environment on earth is the internet. Through social media, we have come to find that the six degrees of separation are in full effect. This is the idea that all people are six or fewer social connections away from each other.

There is a game called Six Degrees of Kevin Bacon or Bacon's Law in which players challenge each other to choose an actor whom they connect to another actor via a film in which both actors appeared. This is repeated to try to find the shortest path that leads to prolific American actor Kevin Bacon. It rests on the assumption that anyone involved in the Hollywood film industry can be linked through their film roles to Bacon within six steps.

Taking this into the six degrees of separation, Richard is only 2 degrees from Kevin Bacon because his brother was an extra in Bacon's film, "Footloose."

Just as Heather was able to move into an area where she knew no one but was still able to put a post on social media and get local people to come help lay their sod, so it is that we are never more than six people from what connection we may need. If you don't believe us, test it out.

Therefore, it's important to pay attention to our near connections—treating the people in our lives, our neighborhoods, and our communities with respect and care. But we also need to pay attention to our further connections—those we know through the internet and other forms of global communication. Treating people, groups, or communities that we may never actually meet with contempt, cruelty, or unjust criticism has an eventual ripple effect. We may not see the consequences immediately, but the harm those attitudes create will eventually affect our personal experiences and our connections.

In a world that is more electronically connected than at any time in human history, taking care to treat connections we experience indirectly with the same amount of respect, kindness, and dignity we use in our direct experience is an important principle of connection.

Principle Six—A Connection is a connection is a connection

Lately, we've come across some research on the real phenomenon of "imaginary friends." It's been said that children with imaginary friends are usually sociable, imaginative, and empathetic. They may also be better at imagining how others think and feel. There are a lot of benefits to having imaginary friends.

While neither of us had an imaginary friend personally, Christine's brother had an imaginary dog when they were kids. Stymy, as he called him, went everywhere with them. He joined them on family outings and meals. Likewise, we've probably all had at least one friend who had an imaginary friend in early childhood. These imaginary friends gave them courage, kept the monsters away, and aided them in some of the challenges they experienced during that time of childhood. The research indicates that this is not only more common than we might think, but fundamentally more positive than negative. An imaginary friend is not a connection to be mocked—even if it makes no sense to someone who's never had one.

Besides imaginary friends, we often have connections to animals. We've come to find how unique these friendships can be. For some of us it might seem odd when someone dresses up their dog or cat and has them on their Christmas card. For others, this is perfectly understandable. Overall, it's a connection.

We can help each other be better connectors by realizing that a connection or relationship that is less important or even irrelevant to one might be foundational and deeply personal to someone else. The idea of "live and let live" gets even stronger when it doesn't just focus on humans.

Chapter 4 Reflection Questions

What are some expectations I have of others that I've never clearly communicated? What's kept me from communicating those expectations?

What role do unspoken expectations play in the relationships I most want to strengthen?

In what relationships have I stopped showing up fully? Why did I stop?

Chapter 4 Challenge

Choose **one** of the six connection principles from this chapter that stands out to you—maybe it spoke to a current situation, reminded you of a strength, or challenged you to think differently. Then:

1. Name the Principle

Which principle are you choosing to focus on? (*Example: "Connection helps us thrive in harsh environments."*)

2. Take a Small Action

Do one thing this week that reflects that principle. What will you do? (*Ideas: Reach out for help, stand up for something that matters, reconnect with an old friend.*)

3. Reflect

How did it feel to apply this principle in real life?

What did you learn or notice about connection?

Chapter 5:

The Beginning of Becoming a Great Connector

In order to become excellent connectors and develop deeper relationships, we need to understand what causes us to disconnect in the first place.

Disconnection doesn't usually happen all at once. It's more often a slow drift than a sudden break—a missed moment here, an unspoken hurt there. Over time, everyday stress, unresolved tension, and emotional withholding quietly chip away at closeness. We get busy, distracted, or overwhelmed. We assume the other person knows how we feel or what we need. We avoid hard conversations or retreat into silence, thinking it will protect the relationship—but in reality, it builds walls.

At the heart of disconnection is usually a deep unmet human need: the need to feel seen, heard, valued, and safe. When any of those needs aren't acknowledged—when we stop being present, stop being curious, stop communicating with intention—connection withers. The good news? Disconnection isn't final. It's a signal, not a death sentence. And when we learn how to recognize the signals, we can begin to rebuild. Becoming a better connector starts with awareness, then choosing to show up differently—with more presence, more empathy, and more courage.

Several years ago, Christine experienced this in her own marriage. Financial pressures, combined with a lack of communication, started to create a strong disconnect between her and her husband. Their communication became the bare minimum—kids, bills, and chores. They had very little to talk about outside of that and most days she felt like she was walking on eggshells.

She remembers thinking to herself, "How did we get here?" She realized there are some basic elements that start to erode relationships:

1. **Unspoken expectations**. Often, we want our partner, friends, family, and even coworkers to read our minds and just know what it is we want or need. These unspoken expectations can start to create resentment when they're not fulfilled. We become bitter and slowly stop communicating.

2. **Avoiding difficult conversations**. For Christine, that was everything. She disliked talking about finances, the kids, or anything that she thought might create contention between her and her husband. The more she avoided the conversation, the more the wedge between them grew.

3. **Assuming rather than asking.** In our humanness, most of us tend to assume the worst rather than just ask to gain understanding and clarification. We jump to conclusions and never really know the truth. We react to the other person accordingly, and often they have no idea what is really going on.

4. **Emotional withdrawal**. This is probably the one that is the hardest when we experience it. We start to shut down. Sometimes it happens because we're simply burned out. But other times it happens because of fear or even apathy. We start to feel like roommates or even strangers.

5. **Lack of appreciation**. Gratitude is a great way to feed a relationship. Without it, the connection starves. When someone doesn't feel appreciated, they withdraw even further.

6. **Breakdown in communication**. This is when frequent criticism, defensiveness, stonewalling, or miscommunication comes in. When these things are a part of our communication, we no longer feel emotionally safe and we shut down.

7. **Stress and life transitions**. Major changes, such as job loss, health issues, or the loss of a parent or sibling, can put extra strain on a relationship and often creates that burnout that we spoke of earlier.

8. **Loss of shared experiences**. The disconnect is solidified when we stop doing things together. We quit going on dates, laughing

together, and we further take each other for granted, just focusing on day-to-day tasks rather than the things that originally drew us together.

Most disconnection doesn't come from a lack of love—even though it might feel that way. It comes from a lack of attention and intention. Busy lives and assumptions made in silence pull us in different directions without us even being aware. When we realize we have disconnected, we first need to determine why. What has caused us to disconnect?

Christine is a certified Canfield Success Principles Trainer and her favorite principle to teach is Success Principle 1: Take 100% Responsibility For Your Life. We will go a little deeper on this later in the book, but what this means is acknowledging that you are the primary creator of your experiences, both good and bad, and that your choices and responses to events directly impact your outcomes. Applied here, it means that you own your part in the disconnect.

The good news is that disconnection doesn't have to mean the end of the relationship. Rather, it's an invitation to re-engage, renew, and reconnect. This isn't about fixing what's broken but about building something stronger than before. And we have noticed in our own relationships that when we put the effort into reconnecting in our marriages, and other important relationships, we do eventually build something much stronger and more joyful.

We all want to build greater and stronger connections with our family members– spouse, children, siblings, parents, and even in-laws. We might even want to be better connectors with our neighbors and coworkers. To achieve that goal, we need to activate four insights into our daily lives.

Here are some simple insights to get you started on the path to reconnection (or to strengthening an existing connection to avoid disconnect):

The insights are:

1. *Challenge where you start.* There are many approaches out there that tell us where to start on improving a specific

connection. We'll **recommend** one starting point that works in any situation.

2. *Challenge what you want.* The type or degree of connection you're working toward matters. For example, I want the highest and deepest connection with my spouse, and then my children. But I also want connection with my neighbors and community but in ways which require different investments of effort.

3. *Challenge what you see.* Sometimes the biggest barrier to improving connection with a specific person grows out of our Belief Windows, or how we see that person. Our paradigm is affected by our history with them, our expectations for and of them, their strengths and weaknesses, and our strengths and weaknesses. We'll share a simple but powerful tool for analyzing how you see this person. This tool will help you make some course corrections that will help you correctly adjust your paradigm and thus energize your approach to improving your connection.

4. *Challenge your approach.* Finally, we'll share a **Connection Investment Plan** that will help to guide your connection efforts. This Plan will include a specific framework as well as tools to bring image boards, journaling, and other resources into your connection toolkit.

We don't always recognize when our connections are withering or fading. If we don't evaluate frequently, we often don't see the disconnect until it is almost too late. It starts with missed phone calls, quiet tension, and those moments when you want to reach out, but don't. It leads us to feeling overwhelmed, sad, confused, and even lonely. We want to connect, but we don't know how to rebuild that closeness. Whether it's trying to connect with a child who's pulled away, wanting to have more emotional intimacy with your spouse, or reconnect with a friend who's detached themselves, the desire is the same: to have a deeper connection.

Wanting to connect and knowing how to build it are two very different things. That's why this section exists—to provide a flexible roadmap that helps you understand where connection thrives, where it weakens, and how to reawaken it.

Let's put this into action.

First, for this to work you need to "pick a person" that you'd like to build a stronger connection with. This could be a person in your immediate family (spouse, child) or extended family (parent, sibling), a friend, or even someone at work. Consider why you want to build a deeper connection. In order to keep you motivated to continue the work, it's important to understand your reasons.

Note: Once you learn how to improve your connection, you can apply these same insights to any relationship in your life.

The Connection Core

We know that human connection is vital to our health and well-being. We have a deep desire to understand and be understood. And sometimes we have a connection that used to be there, but now it's gone. Other times, we want to connect with someone new, and they may not seem as open to it. That desire to *break through*—to close the gap between us and someone we care about—is something almost all of us have felt.

Sometimes that resistance we feel from the other person is unintentional. Maybe they don't even realize we're trying to reach out. Other times, it's more deliberate—they're hesitant, disinterested, or even actively avoiding connection. No matter what the cause, the effect can be deeply painful.

You might have found yourself thinking:

- *You don't see me.* I feel invisible to you. My efforts to connect go unnoticed.

- *You don't want more from me.* You're content with the level of connection we have, even if I'm not.

- *You don't want me in your life.* You're pulling away—or keeping me out entirely.

Here's the truth: trying to connect with someone who feels distant is hard. It's vulnerable. It can stir up all kinds of doubt and heartache. And yet—when that person truly matters to you—the risk of reaching out is almost always worth it. Even if the connection only improves a little. Even if it takes time. Even if the only shift is inside *you*.

We've all seen what happens when you throw a pebble into a very still pond—a series of ripples move out from where the stone landed, getting larger and larger in dimension as they move away from the initial "splash."

Imagine that the initial "splash" when the stone breaks the surface of the water as your sincere attempt to "break through" with the person you've chosen for this section. You're the pebble, and the water with its initial "surface tension" is the relationship as it exists now. What you'd like to do is positively affect that surface tension in such a way that your connections ripple out from the initial contact and become larger and more meaningful as the ripples move across the surface.

Keep that idea in your mind and let's compare those ripples to our relationships. The stone hits the middle and then each ripple will represent one of these principles.

Ripple 1: Challenge where you start

This is your emotional "why." It's what you hope for the future and what leads you to move forward in that relationship. Whether we have a sure vision, or just an idea in our minds of what we think that future should be, the vision we have for this person or relationship exists within us.

But why call it a vision? Because it is about seeing something. This vision allows us to see our ideal future and how our goals fit together. It gives energy to what we're doing right now because we can see the connection between the everyday things we're working on, and something bigger and grander.

But often this vision isn't necessarily "shared," which creates contention, unmet expectations, and disconnection.

There's a comic strip by Charles Schwartz that has a picture of Charlie Brown and Snoopy in camping gear and a message that reads, "Just because my path is different, doesn't mean I'm lost."

How often do we have an idea of the path our children should take in their lives? Or do we feel like we know what's best for our spouse on any given topic? Do we argue about the right way to load the dishwasher or fold the laundry?

It's important that we get an understanding of what that person wants for their life—not just what we want for it. Ask yourself:

- What do you envision for the person you're trying to connect with?
- Have you shared your vision? Have they shared theirs?

Ripple 2: Challenge what you want

Once you understand how your vision differs from that special person's, you can start to come together with a more shared and universal vision that will guide your relationship forward (the WITH space). Connection isn't a one-size-fits-all. Some relationships thrive on closeness and daily interaction. Others need more space, flexibility, or emotional distance. Sometimes we have to evaluate the level of closeness and interaction that's needed based on what we discover.

Christine and her sister are incredibly close as the only girls in their family and only 22 months between them in age. They will talk on the phone almost daily, and love discussing everything from the weather and how work is going to the deepest challenges they're having in their marriages or with their kids.

Her sister, Meg, has a daughter and a son, whereas Christine has five sons. And while their conversations about their kids have a lot of similarities, they also have many differences. Meg feels frustrated that her son isn't always willing or able to check in with her, go to lunch, and spend 1-1 quality time with her now that he's older. Christine has been a parent much longer and has gotten used to that with her boys and has learned to take whatever interaction she can get. It doesn't frustrate her because she understands that's just the way it is with most boys.

Connection has two parts: how close you want to be and how often you want that connection. When those desires don't match, frustration builds as it does for Christine's sister.

Let's try mapping this out. Think about the people in your life—where would you place each one?

- Who do you want frequent, deep connection with?
- Who feels more comfortable with low-key, occasional contact?
- Where is the mismatch and how can you talk about it honestly?

This isn't about forcing closeness. It's about recognizing your needs and theirs and then finding a middle ground where you can both be happy with the level of connection.

Ripple 3: Challenge what you see

When connections are blocked, stagnant or withering, it's usually not the person, it's the window we're looking through.

Let's revisit the Belief Window for a moment. Think of someone you are having a hard time feeling connected to.

Maybe you've labeled them as unreliable, stubborn, or selfish. Maybe they disappointed you once and you've been filtering every interaction through that experience. Maybe they let you down in a time of need, or even betrayed you, and now you're having a hard time trusting them again. The danger is, when we decide who someone is, we stop seeing who they're becoming.

Changing your beliefs isn't easy, but it's possible. It's like that children's story, *"The Little Engine That Could.* The engine had never pulled something that heavy before, but she repeated a new belief: *I think I can.* And as she kept going, it became: *I know I can.*

That's how belief changes work—with practice, repetition, and hope.

Try this: Think about someone you struggle to connect with.

- What do you believe about them?
- Are those beliefs based on current reality—or past pain?
- What would you *like* to believe about them?

Start rewriting the story. Choose a belief that brings hope, even if it's just: *They're trying in their own way.*

Ripple 4: Challenge your approach

Christine and her husband often argue about the best route to take to get to the Texas Roadhouse in their area. He likes to take one way that she thinks overshoots the destination and causes them to backtrack. He thinks it's faster because it avoids a train crossing and an extra stoplight or two. Ultimately, it doesn't really matter which route they take, if they arrive safely to their destination.

In our marriages, our families, and even in relationships with colleagues and co-workers, we often share the same basic desires. We want to be happy, successful, and productive and we want the same for those we are connected to. However, we often have different approaches to achieving those shared desires.

Connection takes more than good intentions—it takes action. That's why we recommend creating a simple **Connection Investment Plan**.

Start by focusing on just one relationship you want to improve.

Ask yourself:

- What kind of relationship do I want with this person?
- Where are we already aligned? (Where are our WITH spaces?)
- Where are we clashing or missing each other?
- What is one small step I can take to close that gap?

You might start by changing the way you show appreciation, asking better questions, making time for shared experiences, or simply softening your tone.

It is exciting when we can find simpler, useful ways to at least initially address complex challenges. Our relationships with others are often very complex, but our message to you is this:

You can assess where you're connected or disconnected by looking in only four places (the ones listed above). And where you find connection, leverage and grow that connection. Where you find disconnection or differences, address those differences. In a world where connections with important relationships are the beginning, there is opportunity for more flexibility in all the other areas. We can have different visions of what a perfect life is. Different missions on how to move forward. Different values to govern our choices and behaviors. Different goals on what to do and when and how to do it. We can make different choices in a day about when to stay on plan and when to flex to a task or new opportunity. In other words, rooted in the profound importance of the relationship, we can give each other grace in all the other ways we can connect or choose to be different.

Committing to building a relationship is the first ripple in the pond. Once you've found that relationship you will notice that the succeeding ripples will often be different than what you would want for yourself or expect from them. But, because the relationship is central and the most valued of everything else in consideration, you will look for and work on ways to maintain connection to that relationship while working through the differences that, if not addressed, could destroy the relationship itself.

Start with relationships. Accept differences. Give grace. Find ways to be WITH each other rather than AGAINST each other.

Chapter 5 Reflection Questions

Think of a person you would like to reconnect with.

What is your "why" for reconnecting with this person? Why does this relationship matter to you right now?

What belief are you currently holding about this person that might be influencing the way you show up with them? Is it still true—or is it time to update it?

What would progress in this relationship look like for you? What's one meaningful step you can make to move the relationship forward?

Chapter 5 Challenge

Begin your journey to becoming a great connector by reflecting on your current relationships and examining where disconnection might be starting *with you*.

1. **Pick One Relationship**
   Choose one relationship in your life that feels distant, strained, or less fulfilling than you'd like. This could be with a friend, family member, coworker, or partner.

2. **Reflect on Your Starting Point**
   Ask yourself:

- *Where did I first notice the disconnection?*

- *What assumptions or expectations might I have brought into this relationship?*

- *Have I pulled back emotionally or mentally? Why?*

3. **Identify One Shift You Can Make**
   Based on what you uncover, choose one thing you can shift—not in the other person, but in yourself. It could be your approach, your tone, your effort, or your mindset.

4. **Do One Small Act of Reconnection**
   This might be a kind text, a compliment, an honest conversation, or just being fully present when you're together. Small steps open big doors.

SECTION 2

Chapter 6:

Personal Connection is About WHAT, Not WHY

There's a business book called *Start with Why: How Great Leaders Inspire Everyone To Take Action* by Simon Sinek. His bestselling book appears to focus primarily on connecting individuals and teams to their organizations. It poses the idea that having a "why" as the reason you do something is a great and important thing. However, asking "why" questions can create contention. Think about it: you ask your son or daughter, "Why are you changing your major?" or your spouse, "Why aren't you applying for that promotion?" or "Why are you wearing that to the party tonight?" What kind of response do you think you're going to get? Probably not a WITH response but more likely a defensive response.

We propose that in personal relationships it is better to start with "What" rather than "Why."

Creating, repairing, or improving a connection or relationship can be challenging. It's always possible that, in the desire to connect and be supportive, we come across as the opposite.

WHY questions, which are natural to ask when you see someone you care about struggling, can feel aggressive, even hostile. So how do we connect AND help without crossing that invisible line?

WHAT questions are helpful without being too nosey or aggressive. The best WHAT questions are those that follow a century old model of human behavior. This model is sometimes called a productivity pyramid, especially when it is looked at through an organizational lens. We're not as focused on productivity in our relationships as we are in creating quality connections for more personal reasons. In doing so, productivity can be one of the powerful products of personal connection. (If you're interested in improving connections in your organizations with the goal to directly impact productivity and other key organizational outcomes, look for our upcoming book: *Connecting: The Leadership Superpower* or go to www.avec-me.com).

The four levels of the traditional pyramid work at a personal level when they are posed as Four Questions, seeking to stimulate Four Connection Conversations.

Those Four Questions are all WHAT…

What matters most to you? (Mission/Vision/Values)

Grade School: "If you could only pick one thing that's super important to you—something that makes you really happy or feels good inside—what would it be?"

Junior High: "What's something in your life right now that really matters to you— something you care about a lot or that feels really important?"

High School/Young Adult: "When you think about your life right now, what's something that truly matters to you, something that really drives you, gives you purpose, or just feels important?"

College Age: "If you had to pick one thing that really matters to you right now—something you truly care about or are focused on—what would it be?"

Adult/20s–30s: "Who or what feels really important to you right now?"

Adult/40-plus: "At this point in your life, what really matters most to you?"

What's something you really want to accomplish? (Goals)

Grade School: "If you could get really good at something or do something awesome this year, what would it be?"

Junior High: "Is there something you're really hoping to get better at or do this year—like a goal you've set for yourself, even if it's just for fun?"

High School/Young Adult: "What's something you're working toward right now—or even just thinking about doing—that feels like a goal for you this year?"

College Age: "What's something you're aiming for right now—whether it's school-related, career stuff, or just something personal you really want to make happen?"

Adult 20s–30s: "What's a goal you're working on—or even just thinking about—that feels meaningful to you right now, whether it's about work, relationships, or life in general?"

Adult 40-plus: "Is there something you're working toward or thinking about these days—whether it's a personal goal, something for your family, or just a change you'd like to make?"

What are you currently doing to accomplish that? (Pathway/Process)

Grade School: "That sounds awesome. What are you doing to get better at it or make it happen?"

Junior High: "That's a cool goal. What steps are you taking to work toward it, or what have you tried so far?"

High School/Young Adult: "That's a solid goal. How are you going about it? What are you actually doing to move toward it right now?"

College Age: "That sounds like an important goal. What kind of steps are you taking to move toward it, or what's been helping you stay on track?"

Adult 20s–30s: "That's a great goal. What are you doing to make progress on it, or what's been helping you stay focused lately?"

Adult 40-plus: "That sounds meaningful. What steps are you taking toward it, or what's been helping you move in that direction lately?"

What are your priorities today? (Daily Activities)

Grade School: "What's something important you're hoping to do today—something that would make you feel proud or happy if you got it done?"

Junior High: "What's one thing you really want to get done today that feels important to you—something that would make the day feel like a win?"

High School/Young Adult: "What's one thing you're hoping to accomplish today that actually feels meaningful or like it'll move you forward in some way?"

College Age: "What's one thing you really want to get done today that feels important—whether it's for school, work, or just for yourself?"

Adult 20s–30s: "What's one thing you're hoping to check off today that actually matters to you—something that would make the day feel worthwhile?"

Adult 40-plus: "What's one thing you're hoping to get done today that really matters—whether it's for you, your family, or just peace of mind?"

The 5th Question

Once this conversation is underway and you are listening with a real intent to understand, you will follow up with the 5th Question:

What can I do to support you?

(Meaning what can I do to support you in what matters most to you, your goals, your processes, or your daily priorities—you can build on any one area or combination.)

Once you understand the things that matter most, and what they want to do to move them closer to those things, you are in the position to offer support. The key is to follow through with that **5th Question**.

Sometimes you may have to establish or reinforce boundaries to that support and possibly deny some requests. We will talk about how to make those decisions in an upcoming chapter. As much as possible, try to support them in the way they want your support rather than in the way you feel you should give it. And remember, advice isn't always what they're looking for.

We've identified four ways to BE supportive:

- BE curious—Talk WITH. (What would you like to talk about?)
- BE available—Work WITH. (How can I be there for you?)
- BE creative—Build WITH. (Do you want some help on details or options?)
- BE near—Walk WITH. (Do you just need me to be here for you?)

Once you know WHAT they need from you and have an idea of how you can BE supportive and find those WITH spaces, then go to work and watch your connection grow.

Now let's dive deeper into the 4 BE's and find our WITH spaces.

Chapter 6 Reflection Questions

When I've asked WHY questions in the past, how were they received? Did they build connection or defensiveness?

What's one relationship I could deepen this week using the WHAT question framework?

How would my relationships change if I focused more on asking instead of assuming?

Chapter 6 Challenge

Step 1: Start a "WHAT" Conversation

Use some variation of the following questions based on their age and your relationship:

- What matters most to you right now?

- What's something you're working toward?

- What are you doing to move closer to that goal?

- What's one thing that feels important to do today?

- What can I do to support you?

Step 2: Practice One of the Four BE's

Based on what they share, choose how you'll show up:

- **BE Curious.** Ask open-ended questions.

- **BE Available**. Offer time or presence.

- **BE Creative**. Brainstorm with them.
- **BE Near**. Simply stay present and listen.

Step 3: Reflect

Did the conversation feel different than usual?

What surprised you?

How did they respond to your support?

Remember: Connection grows when we stop trying to fix and start trying to understand. Asking WHAT shows care. Showing up WITH shows love.

Chapter 7:
The BE Tools

We've all had experiences crossing the street, either as a child with a parent or other adult, or as an adult with a child. It was natural to tell the child, "Hold my hand" as we prepared to cross. We would teach them to look both ways before crossing. Safety was the number one goal in getting them and you across the road safely.

Almost two decades ago Robert Fulghum released a global bestseller titled, *"All I Really Need to Know I Learned in Kindergarten."* That book contains a list of simple rules that most of us did learn in early childhood which still have powerful applications in adult life.

One of my favorite rules from the book is:

When you go out into the world, watch out for traffic, hold hands, and stick together.

In building relationships and deepening our connections, we have an opportunity to be WITH those people. We call these opportunities to connect "WITH spaces." We can talk WITH, work WITH, build WITH, and walk WITH those that we are connected to.

When we look at being supportive of the people in our lives, WITH spaces is a life-altering idea. It's an idea that helps to shape the process of finding, enhancing, and sustaining human connections. We're going to look at four connection behaviors that create and expand where we're WITH each other and guide us as we learn to support each other. These behaviors are simple, but powerful, like Fulghum's rules in his book. You can learn them and apply them immediately. You may recognize and see things you're already doing that are helping you connect with others. And, unless you're already perfect, we hope that you'll see opportunities for continued change and growth.

All four behaviors, which we call the BE-haviors, not only help us in our communication but also remind us that when you go out into the world, we need to watch out for traffic, hold hands, and stick together.

BE Curious (Talk WITH)

Do you just want to talk?

A few years ago, Christine purchased a game called "Do You Really Know Your Family?" It's a game in which one player draws a card, reads the statement, and everyone has to guess the answer. The key is to be the player who knows the other players the best. They played it after Thanksgiving, and everyone had a lot of fun while also getting to know each other better!

Christine and Richard have both always loved asking questions and getting to know people. Curiosity in relationships is important because it helps deepen connections, builds understanding, and fosters growth. It helps us develop a "WITH" space with those people.

Often, when we talk to others, our interactions tend to fall somewhere along a continuum from talking AT them (one-sided) and talking WITH them (both or all parties are participating).

We grew up in a world where adults talked AT children who listened and did what they were told (well, until we were teens). There was a saying, "Children are to be seen, not heard." There was very little experience of talking WITH adults. As children, our communication experiences with adults were primarily passive.

Talking AT someone has its place, such as when we are giving instructions. However, if we aren't more intentional about choosing the best approach for the situation, talking AT someone will diminish opportunities to talk WITH someone. And when we talk WITH, we become more connected—we are WITH them, not just in conversation, but also in heart.

Let's take a somewhat common example:

You're preparing dinner and one of your children asks to help. You hand them a potato and ask them to cut it up. You go by to check up on them and notice the potatoes are in various shapes and sizes—some large and some very small. Knowing that this will cause the potatoes to cook unevenly, you have two ways to approach this:

Talk AT them by immediately correcting them and telling them they're doing it all wrong.

Or... talk WITH them and "BE Curious" by saying something like, "I notice you cut the potatoes into different sized pieces... is there a reason you didn't make them all about the same size?" To which they respond, "You said to cut them up, you didn't say they need to be the same size."

How often have you found yourself talking AT your spouse, child, or even a friend when it should've been a WITH conversation? What kept you from being curious and asking questions? We tend to do this in our everyday conversations, while we focus on what we want to say next rather than listening with the intent to understand. We do it during disagreements, while parenting, and on social media!

To really connect and be WITH someone, we have to talk WITH them. Communication is key. The need to want to know and understand your spouse, your child, or your colleague better requires active listening and self-awareness.

Notice how you can pivot to "instruction" without it diving into Talk AT and control mode. "You're

right, I forgot to suggest that they should all be nearly the same size. Any idea why I might

want that?" They reply (somewhat sarcastically), "Because you're a control freak?"

"Well," you say, "that might be true sometimes but not in this case. We want all the potatoes to cook evenly so some aren't raw and others mushy and tasteless. To help them cook uniformly we cut them to the same size. Does that make sense?"

There is a temptation to pivot into talk AT (high instruction or telling mode) when we see someone not performing the way we expect. To find the WITH space it's our goal to temper our instruction to BE Curious as to why they're doing things the way they are.

BE Curious is the choice that helps us balance Talk AT (low experience, so a need for high instruction/guidance) with Talk WITH (high experience, so less need for instruction/guidance). At the root of these choices is your desire to CONNECT with the person. You don't want to frustrate them with unnecessary early failure because you didn't give them enough instruction or guidance. Nor do you want to frustrate them with micromanaging when their ability to do what is needed is clearly there.

BE Available—Work WITH

How can I be there for you?

The majority of Christine's career was spent in real estate. Her main focus was working with first-time homebuyers. There were occasions when she helped someone sell a home and buy a new one. Her husband spent the majority of his career in moving and storage. This meant they had a lot of commonalities in the things they saw in the work they did.

They discovered early on that moving is one of the most stressful and emotionally complex experiences a person can go through. It affects multiple areas of life: mental health, emotional well-being, financial stability, and even identity when we are leaving the familiar for the unfamiliar. Add to that the fact that most humans struggle with change and we can see how this puts pressure on us and on our relationships.

There are a lot of things that have to get done. When working with clients who were selling a home, there was the all-important Herculean effort of prepping the house for sale. Then there was the challenge of keeping it "perfect" for showings (and God bless the family with children that have to live in a home that has to stay "perfect"). Added to that comes the stress of hoping it gets shown and that a decent offer comes in and then navigating the remainder of the process while it is inspected and the buyer gets final approval for the loan.

Then there are all the things that come with the relocation, whether down the street, to another state, or even overseas. There's the organizing and planning, probably looking for a new home to purchase or rent, and the packing and moving, which brings its own set of challenges because there are so many moving parts. Often, we try to do it all on our own, either because we don't want to ask for help (feeling like people aren't really available), or we're hoping someone will see the need for help and offer—and then when they don't, we grow resentful. We can lose ourselves, our patience, and our perspective in the turmoil and tasks, as well as the unmet and unexpressed expectations. This causes our relationships to suffer.

BE Available, the second of the WITH tools, is rooted in the chaotic balance of working ON that

list while working WITH the people in your life that need your attention—often right now. And… it isn't like you can just put one of the options aside ("I'll handle the move list later" or "our children are just going to have to look after themselves for a couple of days"). Both are critical, both are urgent.

Relationships are the most important "option" when conflicts occur. By prioritizing the relationship, we can better navigate and determine the best way to resolve conflict. But there are items on the to-do list that are important to get done as well. Richard has found the best way to manage this real-world challenge is to run his to-do list against the "D check" so he can, hopefully, free up time to invest in BE-ing Available to the important people in his life.

The D Check

The D check works this way: everything on your to-do list sorts into one of the following buckets or categories:

Do It. These are the things that have to be done today. Do It items have two characteristics: they can only be done by you, and they must be done sooner rather than later.

Delay It. These items still fall into the "must be done by me" category but they can be delayed by hours or days, maybe even longer.

Delegate It. This is where you're going to ask for help. In business this is often formalized. In life, it's more of, "Can you please help me?"

Drop It. There are things on most to-do lists that, if we're really honest with ourselves, are "nice to do" rather than "necessary to do." When we are dealing with a lack of time or bandwidth, these "nice to do" items should get dropped.

The goal driving the "D List" is to free up time from working on the list to **Working WITH** an important person or persons in your life. By releasing yourself from having to do everything, you can free up time to be there for the most important people in your life. You can focus on WITH activities including mentoring, listening, supporting, and spending quality time with someone who needs you. In **BE-ing Available** to **Work WITH** someone, it's important you discover how they want or need you to be there for them.

The enemy of *being available* isn't the to-do list itself. It's the belief that we are somehow superhuman—that we can work *on* everything that demands our attention and, at the same time, work WITH everyone in our lives who wants or needs our time and attention, which often keeps us from BE-ing Available when it's needed the most.

At a logical level, we know this is impossible. Yet, counter to that logic, we all know someone who—*when observed from the outside*, without knowing everything that's going on behind the scenes—*seems* to be superhuman. There are superhuman moms and dads, superhuman professionals and experts at work, superhuman bosses, business owners, and entrepreneurs.

There are superhuman kids that our kids compare themselves to. And we do this as adults, without knowing what is going on in their lives and behind their outward appearance.

Superhuman or Super Connector

What if, instead of trying to be a superhuman "something" we begin to sort our Work ON list? Let's reconsider our D Check and carefully consider what we can let go of so that we can invest time in being a Super

Connector? The healthier our relationships are, the more likely we are to get support or help in making these important things happen.

There's a woman in Richard's neighborhood who seems to be balancing it all—career, large family, husband, new home, continuous learning, service in her community and church. She is not a superwoman. And she is the first to admit it. But she is a super example of relationship-based decision-making. She has learned that when someone needs her help, she finds a little time to help. And she does so willingly, positively, and regularly.

And, since she's not superhuman there are times when she also needs help. Sometimes she asks and sometimes her friends just know. Regardless of whether she asks or her friends offer, she never waits until people are willing to help. People who are also buried in their own relationships and overflowing to-do lists. Why do people find the time for her? Because she found the time for them.

To BE Available more often, you have to prioritize and sometimes make a different choice. You may use the D List we shared earlier. Or you may just decide to put relationships first—Working WITH people before you Work ON your lists. Whatever approach you take, the outcome we're looking for is the same: you are building relationships by increasing (even a little bit) your Working WITH time by BEing AVAILABLE a little more often today than yesterday.

BE Imaginative—Build WITH

Do you want some help with details or options?

When the support we need includes things like ideas, creativity, and help to figure out details or options, we like to go to imagery. Using our imagination is a great way to get our creative juices flowing and come up with new, out-of-the-box ways of seeing things and approaching situations.

There are different ways to foster our imagination so we can create and come up with new ways and new ideas, and make things happen. One of the ways we've been able to foster our creative juices is through the power of vision boards and visualization.

Christine was introduced to the concept of vision boards in her late 30s. She loves using vision boards and visualization exercises in her own life as well as in the work she does. Visualizing what you want, and the end result, is one of the keys to accomplishing the things we are passionate about and bringing what we want into reality. There is power in that vision! Imagination creates the possibility, then visualization puts it into motion.

Visualization works because of focus and repetition—this isn't magic, it's science. Our brain has a "goal filter" called a Reticular Activating System (RAS). It's a bundle of nerves at the base of the brainstem and it filters the millions of stimuli you encounter every second, allowing only what your brain deems relevant to reach your conscious awareness. That's why when someone you know buys a new car, you suddenly see that same make, model, and color everywhere!

Neuroscience confirms that visualization can **build neural pathways** and prime the brain to recognize opportunities that align with the imagined outcome. When you visualize what you want—such as having a happy relationship, or deepening a connection—on a consistent basis, the RAS starts prioritizing information and opportunities that align with that pursuit. Therefore, what you focus on, your brain starts to look for.

We've noticed in our children and grandchildren that, when it comes to their vision, they have three precious gifts: energy, imagination, and innocence. They are ready to help (energy), they've got their own great ideas (imagination), and they're not yet cynical enough to approach every new or visionary idea with the "oh, that won't work" attitude (innocence).

So, to BE Imaginative using Childlike Visioning we can:

- Start with Energy. Imagine approaching them, being asked to help. How would you communicate your "energy" and excitement to be part of building with them? What kind of things would you say? What type of emotion would you want to convey?

- Embrace Innocence. There were many people who "pooh-poohed" the idea of a smartphone before Steve Jobs pushed (some would say drove) his vision to reality. There were a lot of critics of chicken nuggets before they became THE MOST POPULAR KIDS' FAST FOOD IN THE WORLD!

Even when you see flaws or challenges in a vision, you can maintain honest support for it. How can you communicate improvement without killing the vision?

BE Near—Walk WITH

Do you just need me to be here for you?

The final BE-havior in this part of the story is BE Near which is all about making the adjustments in our own behaviors, motivations, and destinies to STAY WITH those we care about.

Richard has a dear friend who is not only one of the best dads he knows but is one of the greatest marathon runners of all time (even though he's not in any record books). Years ago, Richard's friend Jim, his wife, and their five children all decided to run a marathon as a family. The kids ranged in age from young teenagers to young adults. They trained and trained as a family until it was time to run the actual marathon.

The marathon they chose to run was in St. George, Utah. St. George runs their marathon in October. It's a desert, so the air is dry, and the route is at altitude starting at 5,240 feet in the Pine Valley Mountains. It then descends 2600 feet including one monster hill between miles 16 and 24. The temperature at the start of the race can be as cold as 38 degrees Fahrenheit and go up to the mid 80's by the end. In other words, this is a tough run.

When the race started, the family, as a unit, broke out of the pack. And that's when Jim's training kicked in and he found himself running way ahead of his family. Because this was a family run, he slowed his pace so they could all catch up. After many miles the differences in training and endurance kicked in and the younger kids struggling to keep going.

So, dad dropped back and ran beside each child; he encouraged and pushed them to keep going; he helped them stay the course. Jim did this multiple times: run, get too far ahead, drop back, drop even further back to run with a child, bring them forward, then repeat—over and over.

Their family, all of them, finished the St. George marathon. They set no records, but they all finished. It's amazing to consider that with all the back and forth, Jim probably ran the marathon twice. A marathon can be grueling. Can you imagine running it twice in one day?

This is the essence of BE-ing connected. It is rooted in a commitment to never get too far ahead or fall too far behind those people in your life that need you to STAY WITH ME.

We can fall into the trap of losing connection with others if we are not both sensitive to and willing to adjust our own vision, goals, and aspirations to include them. There is a place in life for individual achievement, for breaking out of the pack and setting a new standard, raising the bar, or disrupting the norm. But, when it comes to relationships, there is also a time to adjust the pace—slow down if we're getting too far ahead or speed up if we're holding them back. If we are prioritizing relationships more than outcomes, then when we get "there," whatever the goal or destination is, is not as important as WHO we get there with.

Chapter 7 Reflection Questions

Which of the BE Tools comes most naturally to you—and which one do you need to grow into?

When was the last time you truly "walked WITH" someone—matching their pace emotionally or relationally? What difference did it make in the way you feel about the relationship?

What's one simple way you can be more present, curious, or available to someone important to you this week?

Chapter 7 Challenge

For this chapter, focus on intentionally practicing each of the four BE tools—one per day, then reflect at the end of the week:

1. **Be Curious.** Initiate a conversation by asking someone a thoughtful *what* question (e.g., "What's been on your mind lately?"). Listen without interrupting or correcting.

2. **Be Available.** Choose one relationship and offer your presence without distraction. Put your phone down, clear your schedule, and *just be there*.

3. **Be Imaginative.** Solve a small problem with someone instead of for them. Brainstorm creative ways to support them *with* their goal or struggle.

4. **Be Near**. Offer quiet companionship to someone going through a hard time, without the need to fix it. Just be WITH them.

Which of these "BE" tools came most naturally to you? Which was hardest—and why? How did others respond to your efforts?

Chapter 8:
Managing the "One-Sided" Connection

Since we don't live in a perfect world, we want to address the reality that sometimes we work hard to build connections, but they still end up feeling one-sided.

Here's a real-world example:

Christine decided to ask her husband the five connection questions. While their marriage is a solid relationship, in her opinion, it doesn't always seem as fulfilling as it could be. Maybe it's just the age and stage of life that they're in, but she wanted to deepen the intimacy that comes from deeper levels of communication. As he answered the questions, Christine immediately began to feel frustrated. Maybe it was partly because he wasn't answering them the way she thought he should, and maybe it was partly because he didn't fully understand what was being asked, but her immediate thought was, "This doesn't work, so now what do I do?"

We asked over 100 people these five questions, and while it worked MOST of the time (98%), there were times when it just didn't "click" for a number of reasons, including the person answering not being open and honest or there was some other barrier preventing connection.

Sometimes in relationships, it feels like we are the only ones "rowing the boat." And when you're the only one rowing, you quickly get burned out and end up going in circles rather than moving forward. So, if you can relate to this in any of your relationships, then this chapter is for you!

As we go through this chapter, we want to remind you of the principle we discussed in Chapter 5 called Taking 100% Responsibility For Your Life. As mentioned, this is the first Success Principle from the book *The Success Principles* by Jack Canfield, and Christine's favorite principle to teach, because it lays the foundation of everything else that we experience in life.

Taking 100% responsibility means **owning your thoughts, actions, reactions, and outcomes**—without blaming others, making excuses, or waiting for someone else to fix things.

It doesn't mean that *everything* that happens is your fault. But it **does** mean that how you **respond** to what happens is within your control.

There seems to be a growing separation of extremes. On one hand are those who are "victims" of everything that happens to them (in other words they take no responsibility). On the other hand, there are those who are worrying about or taking responsibility for things that are not the result of anything they've said or done.

You can stop using reactive language, such as:

- "I can't help it; that's just the way I am."
- "If my boss/spouse/kids were different, I'd be happy."
- "There's nothing I can do."

And instead start using proactive language by asking:

- "What can I learn from this?"
- "What can I do differently next time?"
- "How can I take the next step forward?"

There's a simple formula taught by Jack Canfield that is Christine's go-to whenever she's experiencing something she doesn't want. It's $E + R = O$.

Event (or Experience) + Response = Outcome.

You may not control the event that has you upset or less than satisfied, but you can always control your response (which is one of the only things we can control) and this will ultimately determine the outcome. What it does best is move us out of victimhood and into ownership and empower us to take charge of our lives and our experiences, including our relationships.

Christine has always been interested in personal development, and because of that interest certain things have become easier for her. Communication and expressing her feelings are two of those. Her husband, however, doesn't have the same interest in personal development as Christine does, so this is new territory for him.

After the frustration with her husband died down, Christine did some self-reflection, and she decided to challenge and change that belief on her window. Rather than remaining upset at his answers, she began to see it as a different way of communicating. While she was processing what he was saying and making it about her, the reality was he was just trying to express what he needed in the partnership WITH her.

Sometimes the biggest challenges in our seemingly one-sided connections are really more about dissimilar communication styles. Have you ever talked to someone and you're trying to explain something to them, and they just don't seem to get it? And you keep trying in the same way to explain it, like somehow, they're going to magically understand it this third or fourth time? Here's a novel idea: when you can't get your point or message across, try changing your method.

So, here are some basic communication skills that might assist you when you feel like you're doing all the work:

1. **Adopt curiosity over defensiveness.**

    We've talked about BE-ing Curious. Learn to ask questions to help make sure you're on the same page and to recognize where the miscommunication lies, such as "Can you help me understand what you mean?" Or "What were you feeling when you said that?" This is about showing that you're willing to bridge the gap instead of widening it.

2. **Use "I" statements to clarify your intentions.**

   Saying things like "You never listen" or "You really hurt me" put the other person in a defensive position. Instead, try expressing what you're feeling (again taking 100% responsibility for your experience) by saying things like "I am not feeling heard, can we try to discuss this?" or "I feel hurt when you go play golf after work without checking in with me first." This reduces blame and invites collaboration rather than conflict.

3. **Assume good intent.**

   The truth is that most people are doing the best they can with what they know, and where they're at. When emotions are high, we tend to assume the worst. We let past experiences (maybe even experiences with other people) dictate the outcome, rather than staying in the moment and assessing the situation from a lens that may not be accurate. Try starting with the belief that the other person isn't trying to hurt you, but rather they're trying to be heard and understood too.

4. **Clarify definitions.**

   The words we use are powerful and meaningful and yet can mean different things to different people. For example, what is respect? That can look different to me than it does to you. Even asking someone to be "on time" can mean different things. Growing up, we had to be at least 10 minutes early or we weren't on time, whereas others feel like as long as they arrive within 30 minutes, they have arrived on time. Our childhood experiences have often shaped our understanding of certain words. So, ask: "What does that word mean to you?" That way you can ensure you are eliminating additional confusion.

5. **Slow down the conversation.**

   When we are in the middle of a heated conversation, two things tend to happen: one, we raise our voice and two, we start talking faster. When this happens, we want to turn it down and slow it down. Be intentional about this so that you can avoid additional misunderstandings. Simply say, "Can we slow this down? I want to really understand what you're saying." This invites presence over reaction. Additionally, if the person you're wanting to connect with takes more time to process things, this will make it feel more inclusive and provide them with an opportunity to be proactive.

6. **Mirror and validate.**

    You may have heard this before, and it's a great Neuro Linguistics Programming (NLP) practice as well. When you feel like you're not being heard or validated, then try making sure the other person is being heard and validated. Often what we give is what we get (maybe not in exact measures, but it's a great start). Try repeating back what you think they have said so you have mutual understanding. "What I hear you saying is…. Is that right?" Even if you're wrong, it invites the other person to clarify what they're trying to say, and they now feel validated and seen.

7. **Name the pattern together.**

    If you feel that your miscommunications are common occurrences and you continue to get nowhere, try zooming out instead of looking at it so closely. Christine's dad would use the phrase, "You can't see the forest through the trees." Try saying something like, "I've noticed we keep having the same kind of miscommunication. I don't want that for us. What do you think is going on?" Naming the pattern invites joint ownership instead of blaming.

If, after trying all this, you still feel like you're in it alone, then it may be time to re-evaluate your boundaries. A simple guide, we've mentioned earlier, is:

- What am I willing to do?
- What am I not willing to do?
- What do I think would be best for everyone involved?

But let's go deeper, in case this process isn't doing it for you. It's important to set boundaries with people in a way that invites understanding rather than conflict. So, here's a little step-by-step guide to do that:

1. Get clear on what you're feeling. Take some time to reflect before addressing the issue to determine what might be causing what you're experiencing.

    - Are you feeling resentful, exhausted, unappreciated?
    - What tasks or emotional efforts do you feel you are carrying alone?
    - What do you wish they would do more of? Or less of?

2. Define what you are and are not willing to do by asking yourself:

    - What am I willing to keep doing in this relationship?
    - What am I not willing to do anymore if things don't change?

3. Have a boundary conversation calmly and honestly. This can be difficult. Especially because we often anticipate the other person's response without really knowing how they will react. Let go of past experiences and go in with a fresh perspective. Then use "I" statements, as mentioned before. For example:

    - "I've been feeling overwhelmed and stretched thin because I've been managing a lot on my own. I really value our relationship, and I need to set some limits, so I don't burn out."
    - "I feel undervalued and unappreciated when I am the one always calling to make plans with you. I value our friendship, and I hope we can have more reciprocity in maintaining it."

> Be honest, not harsh. You're not attacking them, after all, you're just protecting your energy and inviting collaboration.

4. Be specific about the changes you need. Boundaries aren't just emotional lines; they're requests for different behavior. For the examples above, try stating changes like this:

    - I need us to split dinner prep 50/50 during the week.
    - I need you to initiate some of our plans.

5. Hold the boundary with kindness and consistency. This can be hard, because most of us find it easier to move the boundary than to maintain it and deal with possible conflict. If the person resists, remember that pushback doesn't mean the boundary is wrong, it just means they were benefiting from the imbalance. Try saying:

    > "I understand this feels different, but this is what I need to feel good in our relationship."

    Keep the focus on your needs.

Finally, watch for change, or a lack of it. If the other person responds with care and effort, then that's a great sign. If they dismiss you, guilt-trip you, or repeatedly ignore your boundaries, you may need to reassess whether the relationship is sustainable. Not all relationships will go the distance. However, boundaries are both bridges and filters. They help healthy relationships grow stronger, and unhealthy ones to reveal themselves.

Setting a boundary doesn't mean shutting someone out, it's simply saying, "I want to stay in this with you, but not at the cost of losing myself." That's a powerful act of love for both of you.

Chapter 8 Reflection Questions

Where in your life are you currently feeling like you're doing all the relational "rowing"?

When someone doesn't engage with you the way you'd hoped, do you tend to blame them, yourself, or withdraw altogether?

What's one small step you could take this week to shift a one-sided connection toward balance—or toward closure?

Chapter 8 Challenge

For this chapter, take a deeper look at a relationship that feels one-sided. Instead of retreating or blaming, choose curiosity, clarity, and courage.

Step 1: Reflect Honestly

Ask yourself:

- What am I feeling in this relationship (resentment, exhaustion, hurt)?

- What efforts am I making that feel unreciprocated?

- Have I clearly communicated what I need?

Step 2: Take 100% Responsibility

You may not control the other person's effort, but you can control your **response**. Try applying E + R = O:

- **Event**: What's happening?

- **Response**: How have I reacted? What could I do differently?

- **Outcome**: What do I want to create instead?

Your new response:

Step 3: Set (or Reset) a Boundary

Use this prompt to prepare:

> "I've been feeling ____, and I need ____ to stay healthy in this relationship."

Example: "I've been feeling drained, and I need us to share more responsibility at home."

Your boundary statement:

Remember: Boundaries aren't ultimatums—they're invitations to connect more honestly. By being clear about what you need, you give the other person a real chance to meet you there.

SECTION 3

Chapter 9:
Right, Wrong, Different

As a young adult, Richard lived in England for a while. He developed a friendship with a neighbor, Ben. Ben was older, more mature, and far wiser. The more time Richard spent with Ben, the more Richard learned why he wasn't as good a connector as he wanted to be and realized that there were things he needed to change to be that kind of person.

One afternoon they were going for a walk in their neighborhood. They passed a street where a guy was mixing concrete to do some work on his property. As Richard watched, it struck him as odd that, instead of mixing the concrete in a small mixer or even a bucket, the guy was mixing cement, aggregate and water, right on the road surface, turning it with a shovel.

Richard commented to his neighbor Ben that this method was ridiculous, even primitive, and that where he was from (Canada) they would never mix concrete on the road surface—they'd do it a more "civilized" way.

Ben paused at the end of Richard's self-involved and know-it-all comments and said, "Richard, when you're a little older and, hopefully, a lot wiser, you'll learn that there are three conditions or categories in life: right, wrong, and different. And," he continued, "most of life is just different."

Richard has never forgotten that profound life lesson Ben taught him that day. As he's worked his way through life, running into things that seem odd or even wrong to him, he's considered whether what is bothering him is "wrong" or just "different."

We strongly believe in right and wrong. We think certain things are universally wrong. Abusing another human being is wrong. Period.

Showing grace or kindness to another person (even if they reject kindness or take advantage of that grace) is still right.

Having strong boundaries around right and wrong is important in life. But we also need to remember that not everything has a right or wrong, it is just different. So is considering whether those boundaries need some reconsideration or adjustment. In line with the lesson Ben taught him, Richard has developed his own insight into this "categorization" phenomenon.

"Everything feels black and white—until it involves someone you love."

It's easy to hold strong opinions when they're distant or theoretical. But when an issue becomes personal—when it touches someone we love or a principle we deeply care about—our once-absolute convictions can begin to falter.

That's not weakness; it's an invitation. A moment to pause and ask: *Am I willing to see this differently?*

Christine's friend and colleague, whom we will call Sarah, has always been someone who approaches challenges with a mix of pragmatism and empathy. As a seasoned leader in her field, Sarah has a reputation for helping others navigate tough decisions with grace and understanding. But when it came to her son, Sarah found herself in unfamiliar territory.

Like most parents, Sarah assumed her son would do well in school, get good grades, and graduate with his class. Not graduating was incomprehensible; graduating is just what you do.

However, with a son who struggled with ADHD, Sarah had to change her perspective. She soon realized that what she had once viewed as "laziness" was actually a response to school and subjects he simply wasn't interested in and couldn't focus on.

Her son struggled so much with going to school that it began to make him physically ill. This typically unemotional child would cry and beg not to have to go. They had tried medication and counseling, but nothing changed this anxiety he felt. After many sleepless nights, arguments, and finally a lot of soul searching and prayer, Sarah decided to allow him to drop out of school in the 9th grade, with the agreement that he would get his GED as soon as he turned 16.

Almost everyone she knew thought this was the wrong move and were vocal in their criticism. They advised her to take away the things that brought him joy as a punishment, or to force him to do what they thought was right—stay in school. But Sarah knew that pushing him in that way would push him over the edge, and she was certain that wasn't the right thing for him.

In the long run, Sarah realized that we all have different perspectives, and that doesn't make one person's approach right or another's wrong. We simply have different ways of handling things, and sometimes, a situation requires a different approach because each individual is unique.

And yes, that son is now thriving in his own life, and Sarah knows that decision was the right one for him.

Sometimes, you'll reaffirm what you believed before, but still confident in what's right and what's wrong. Other times, you might adjust, refine, or soften your position.

But the real growth isn't in whether you change or stay the same. It's in the *willingness* to reconsider, to stay open to different ways of seeing.

When we connect with people who come from different backgrounds or life experiences, we realize how varied the world can be. Some of these differences feel familiar; others challenge us.

Learning to work through them—while choosing to maintain respect, invite connection, and strengthen relationships—isn't just the challenge. It's the opportunity of a lifetime.

Often, in an attempt to gain control in our own lives, we find ourselves wanting to control the people around us. In dealing with our children, we justify this control as our responsibility to help them become good and successful adults. And yet, we may find ourselves still trying to control them once they become adults, and even after they have their own family.

We feel we have the right to control our spouse or partner because we made a commitment to become "as one" and that "one" has to be what we want, not what they want, or a compromise of both.

And while we may tend to do this in every type of relationship, those familial relationships are usually the ones we try to control the most since they are the people we have the most vested interest in. Can you relate?

Richard has been studying and following the writings and ideas of Barbara Coloroso for years. She is the author of *Just Because It's Not Wrong Doesn't Make It Right: From Toddlers to Teens, Teaching Kids to Think and Act Ethically,* and introduces a practical framework for parents and educators. Richard has learned to think of some of her key principles when assessing his own or anyone else's behavior in a simple but powerful way: When conflict arises, ask whether the issue is illegal, immoral, or unsafe. If the answer is no to all three, it may be an opportunity to allow autonomy in decision-making, even if it makes you uncomfortable. This approach encourages us and others to take responsibility for our actions and learn from natural consequences, which in turn fosters independence and ethical reasoning.

Many years ago, when Richard's daughter, Rachel, was entering high school, she came to him and said, "I've decided I'm going to pierce my eyebrow and pierce my navel." Having studied this new concept, he asked her some questions. "Are you still planning to get part-time work while in high school?" She responded with a resounding "yes." He then told her, "Then you can't pierce your eyebrow." She wanted to know why, so he let her know, "Old people run the world. Whether right or wrong, they don't like facial piercings." She was upset and said, "Well, that's not fair!" And Richard let her know, "I'm not arguing whether it's right or wrong, good or bad, fair or unfair. I'm just telling you how it currently works, and it will affect your ability to find work."

Rachel, a highly intelligent young woman, felt she'd found the flaw in Richard's approach. "They won't see my navel, " she said (which is true). This was the test for Richard. Is piercing your navel unsafe? Her reply: Not if it's done properly. Is it illegal? Not if an adult gives permission. Is it immoral? That's a personal choice. So, he gave his permission to get her navel pierced. Not what he'd wanted but, in a relationship, sometimes you act or take a stand and sometimes you adapt or let it go.

Coloroso's guidance proved invaluable here. It helped Richard decide what approach to take to a situation that seemed to be headed towards conflict. These three questions are a practical way to "pick your battles." Most importantly it is rooted in ways to stay as connected as possible, even when the going gets difficult.

When it comes to our closest family members, such as spouses or children, we often want to "protect" them, meaning we want to control them—which typically creates friction. By following this simple guide, we can let go and trust what good can come, rather than fear what might go wrong. It's important that we put our faith over our fear and give trust to those with whom we're connected, especially in our most important relationships.

Chapter 9 Reflection Questions

Think about a person and a situation with whom there may be conflict or a conflicting issue arises.

Was their behavior truly wrong—or just different from what you're used to? *(Use Barbara Coloroso's filter: Is it illegal, immoral, or unsafe?)*

Is there a current relationship where perceived control—either yours or theirs—is causing disconnection? What would it look like to shift from control to curiosity?

How might practicing the mindset, "It's not wrong, it's just different," change the way you communicate or connect this week?

Chapter 9 Challenge

For the next three days, choose one conversation, situation, or social media post each day that pushes your buttons—something that you *normally* would label as wrong, irritating, or misguided.

Instead of reacting the way you usually do, do one of the following:

- **Ask a genuine, curious question** instead of making a judgment. *Example: "That's interesting—how did you come to that conclusion?"*

- **Practice Barbara Coloroso's filter**: Ask yourself, "Is it illegal, immoral, or unsafe?" If not, try letting it go—or even allowing it to play out without interference.

- **Do nothing at all.** Literally say nothing. Just observe your thoughts. Can you let someone be different without correcting or fixing them?

Then, at the end of each day, jot down:

- What happened

- What you *wanted* to say or do

- What you *actually* said or did

- How the other person responded

- How it made you feel

Bonus: Choose one relationship (past or present) in which difference led to distance—and reach out to simply reconnect without resolving anything. Just say hello.

Chapter 10:

Living in Parallel

When you've hit a place in a relationship where you can't see eye to eye, the other person won't honor boundaries, or they are just in a constant state of negativity that you can no longer manage, or maybe you just have nothing in common and the relationship has no ability to serve either of you, then it may be time to look at living in parallel.

Not every relationship in our lives is clearly right or clearly wrong for us. Some aren't necessarily toxic or unhealthy—they're just... draining. You might find yourself walking away from a conversation with someone and thinking, *Why do I always feel worse after we talk?* Maybe it's not a harmful relationship, but it's not filling your tank either.

Think about the last time you ran into someone you hadn't seen in ages—maybe a former coworker, an old friend from school, or a parent from when your kids were in preschool together. That brief interaction might have reminded you why you quietly let the connection fade. Not wanting to rekindle every relationship doesn't make you unkind or ungrateful, it makes you human. Being a good person doesn't mean you owe your energy to everyone. It just means you treat others with respect. That's where the idea of *living in parallel* comes in.

Parallel lines never intersect. They move alongside each other but don't cross paths. That's how some relationships are best managed. Living in parallel means you don't seek connection because history tells you it won't be uplifting. But it also means you don't go out of your way to criticize, gossip about, or "unfriend" the other person. You just live your life while quietly wishing them well in theirs.

About seven years ago, Christine went to visit one of her oldest and dearest friends; we'll call her Jane. When they first met, they connected quickly and their friendship continued from there. Christine considered them to be best friends. Jane later moved away and although she had come back "home" to visit a few times, it was Christine's first time going to see her.

Because Jane lived several states away, they hadn't had the type of connection that they had when she lived close. There were no girls' nights out or lunch dates, no sitting at Jane's place and talking for hours. But they did keep in touch regularly through social media and occasional phone calls.

However, when Christine went to visit Jane, it quickly became clear that they were not the same people they'd been for the better part of their friendship. The first two days were okay. They reminisced and saw some of the sights, and then things went downhill.

They ended up getting into a pretty heated argument, which resulted in Christine moving up her flight and leaving a day early. Although it was very tense that last night, and Christine felt incredibly uncomfortable, she felt that eventually they'd talk it out and all would be well. But when she got to the airport, she noticed Jane had completely unfriended and blocked her on all social media platforms.

At first, Christine was crushed. Even though she knew their friendship had grown apart and that in the long run the energy she was using to maintain that friendship could be focused on someone else that she had more in common with, she had refused to let the friendship go.

Since that day, Christine has been able to see how she can live in parallel with Jane. After all, they have a lot of mutual friends. Now Christine is able to hear things about Jane and not be upset or talk badly of her. She simply does exactly what we say to do—she wishes Jane well and moves on with her life. Will their paths ever cross again? It's hard to say. But this idea of living in parallel helps Christine know how she will respond if they do.

There are two types of people we will live in parallel with: people we come into contact with regularly that we have no real connection to, and those that we've had a connection to but have had to take a step away from (like Christine and Jane).

Think about your own life. Who are the people with whom you come into contact? There are neighbors you smile and wave at every morning during the school drop-off rush or colleagues you see on your way to a work meeting. And then there are others who never return a wave, who seem chilly no matter how many warm attempts you make. Who are the people that you've been connected to but now realize you may need to reconsider the connection? Sometimes we try to thaw those frosty relationships. Sometimes we realize we're the only ones trying.

And that's okay. We don't need to carry guilt or spin into *what did I do wrong?* What we can do is choose to live in parallel:

- Be kind.

- Speak gently, or not at all, about them to others.

- Offer a hello now and then, but don't expect connection if it's not mutual.

There's strength—and peace—in setting quiet boundaries that honor your energy without creating conflict.

Richard's grandfather used to say, **"There's no such thing as a weed—it's just a plant growing where you don't want it."** While that might not be entirely accurate (though, fun fact: you can make salads and tea from dandelions and thistles—who knew?), it offers a metaphor for certain relationships in our lives.

Sometimes, we find ourselves entangled in connections that, while not overtly harmful, seem to drain us more than they nourish us. It's akin to a plant thriving in a spot where we'd rather it not be.

Leaving a relationship—be it a long-term partnership, a demanding career, or even the cherished bond with a family member who has passed—is undeniably painful. Sometimes, we make the conscious choice to end these connections; other times, circumstances decide for us. In either scenario, it's natural to grieve, to reminisce, and to hold onto the positive memories that once brought us joy.

However, there are instances when we move beyond healthy remembrance and begin to dwell on the negative aspects. We might find ourselves repeatedly revisiting feelings of anger, betrayal, or resentment. This fixation can become a source of toxic energy, hindering our healing process.

Have you ever known someone—or perhaps recognized in yourself—the tendency to leave a relationship but not truly let it go? Continuously revisiting past grievances, replaying arguments, or harboring resentment? This pattern can be emotionally exhausting and counterproductive.

As we navigate relationships, we sometimes find ourselves entangled in patterns that prevent us from truly moving on. These patterns don't always make a relationship toxic, but they can make it draining, confusing, or emotionally exhausting. Sometimes, we find ourselves staying in relationships because of these invisible forces at play—forces that often keep us stuck in a cycle of hope, guilt, or obligation. Here are a few things to watch out for:

1. **Emotional Attachments That are Hard to Break**: In some relationships, we find ourselves drawn to the person not because of what they bring to our lives now, but because of what we've shared in the past. This attachment can feel as if we're emotionally tied to someone, even when things have clearly changed. It's a common experience to feel like we can't just walk away, even though we know the relationship no longer benefits us.

2. **The Need to Be Needed**: Sometimes, we stay connected to people because we feel responsible for their well-being. This sense of obligation can create an unhealthy dynamic in which our own needs get overlooked. We may find ourselves putting others first, even when it's at the expense of our own happiness. It's important to recognize when we're giving too much of ourselves away, especially when the other person isn't offering the same in return.

3. **The Hope for Change**: In relationships where the other person is unpredictable—kind one moment, distant the next—we often find ourselves holding onto hope. This hope is driven by the expectation that things will change, and that the person we care about will come around. But this can lead to emotional

exhaustion, because it keeps us waiting for something that might never come.

4. **The Fear of Being Alone**: One of the most common reasons we stay in unfulfilling relationships is the fear of loneliness. The idea of being by ourselves can seem scarier than staying in a connection that isn't working. Yet, the truth is that sometimes being alone can be more peaceful than being stuck in a relationship that drains us.

5. **Unmet Emotional Needs**: There are times when we keep seeking fulfillment from a relationship, hoping it will give us the emotional support or validation we crave. But when this need remains unmet, it can lead to frustration, disappointment, and even resentment. It's crucial to recognize when we're relying on someone else to fill a void that only we can truly heal.

6. **Comfort in the Familiar**: Over time, we can become accustomed to the emotional ups and downs of a relationship. It becomes normal, even if it's unhealthy. The familiarity of this dynamic can make it hard to let go because we're used to it, even if it isn't serving us. But breaking free from these habitual patterns allows us to find healthier ways of connecting.

Living in Parallel

Living in parallel with someone means acknowledging these patterns without letting them control your life. It's about making the conscious choice to stop investing emotionally in a relationship that no longer serves you—without guilt, drama, or conflict. You simply acknowledge that the relationship exists, but it's no longer something you're actively trying to fix or change.

Instead of trying to repair the connection, you move on with your life, offering kindness but protecting your energy. **Living in parallel** isn't about abandoning the person or harboring resentment; it's about recognizing the relationship for what it is now and honoring your need to protect your own peace.

So, how can we begin to truly let go and foster healing?

- **Set Boundaries**: Establish clear emotional and physical boundaries to protect yourself from being drawn back into negative dynamics.

- **Seek Support**: Engage with a therapist or support group to process your experiences and develop healthier relationship patterns.

- **Focus on Self-Care**: Prioritize activities and relationships that nurture your well-being and reinforce your self-worth.

- **Reflect on Lessons Learned**: Use the experience as an opportunity for personal growth, identifying patterns to avoid in future relationships.

Remember, healing is a journey, not a destination. It's okay to seek help along the way. Letting go of a negative relationship doesn't mean forgetting the past; it means choosing to prioritize your well-being and future happiness.

Chapter 10 Reflection Questions

Have you ever held on to a connection longer than you should have out of guilt, habit, or obligation?

What's one relationship you've grieved—even though the person is still alive?

How do you differentiate between a challenging but worthwhile relationship and one that has run its course?

Chapter 10 Challenge

For this chapter, take time to evaluate a relationship that feels draining, distant, or forced. Use this challenge to gently assess whether it's time to step back and live in parallel.

Step 1: Identify the Relationship

- Who in your life currently feels more like an emotional weight than a source of connection?

- Do you know if the tension is mutual or mostly internal? (Do you get the sense they are also feeling a similar way?)

- What have you tried to repair or strengthen the relationship?

Step 2: Clarify the Pattern

Ask yourself:

- Do I feel unseen, unheard, or constantly misunderstood in this relationship?

- Do I feel the need to "win" the conversation, prove a point, or fix the other person?

- Am I staying because of guilt, obligation, or fear of being alone?

Step 3: Choose to Let Go Gracefully

If it's time to live in parallel:

- What would "peaceful distance" look like?

- How can you release resentment, while still wishing that person (or group of people) well?

Remember: You don't have to end a relationship to redefine it. Living in parallel is not a failure, it's an act of emotional wisdom. Letting go doesn't mean you no longer care. It means you've chosen to care for yourself, too.

Chapter 11:

Water the Flowers

"Grass isn't greener on the other side, it's greener where it gets the most water."

Life sometimes asks us to live in parallel, side by side with people we care about, even when we don't fully agree. It's not always easy, and it doesn't have to mean distance or disconnection. We want relationships, whether at home or at work, to flourish and deepen whenever possible. Life is more productive and effective when connection is deepened.

That's why we wrote this book. It's filled with practical tools for navigating the real-world mix of blessings and challenges that come with family, friendships, and professional life. Sometimes, taking a stand is necessary—especially when something is unsafe, immoral, or harmful. That's not about control or judgment; it's about honoring what matters most.

Still, whenever possible, look for WITH spaces—the overlap where we can agree, grow, and stay connected. What we've found is powerful: connection is more possible than impossible. And when it happens, the outcomes don't just improve your life—they bless it.

In our relationships, we often find ourselves looking at others when things feel disconnected. We may see a post on social media where a group of friends go out together and we may wonder why our friend group doesn't do things like that. We may see a mother/daughter date and wish we had that type of relationship with our own mother or daughter. We see a husband who appears to dote on his wife or a wife who seems like the perfect career executive and homemaker, and we compare. We wonder if there's something better out there, something we don't have. In reality, we can make what we have just as beautiful and strong as anything we see. We simply need to **nurture it**.

Many years ago, Christine attended a workshop called "Sending the Right Message," hosted by John and Narelle Canaan. During the session, John spoke about the "weeds" we see in the people we are connected to, meaning the flaws or things we don't like about them. We start to hyper-focus on what we perceive as flaws. We see others' actions through a critical lens, picking out the smallest imperfections and magnifying them.

Maybe it's the time they spend scrolling social media instead of engaging with us, or the way they leave things around the house instead of picking them up. You may notice the weight they've gained, thinking they've "let themselves go," or their lack of progress in their career or personal development. You may spot those annoying habits that seem to get under your skin. And before you know it, you are consumed by the "weeds."

When you focus on the weeds, you stop seeing the flowers, the very things that drew you to this person. You forget how they used to surprise you with your favorite drink, or how their sense of humor could turn a stressful day around. You forget their heart, their effort, their goodness. And instead, you zoom in on everything they're doing "wrong."

The Impact of What We Choose to See

This is where positive reinforcement matters more than we think. Dr. John Gottman, one of the top relationship researchers, found that the healthiest couples aren't the ones who never argue, they're the ones who stack up positive moments. His research shows that for every one negative interaction; we need *at least five* positive ones to keep the relationship strong.

Five to one!

Translation: one sarcastic comment about their driving means you've got to balance it out with five "I love how safe you make me feel" kind of moments... or at least one heartfelt compliment and four tacos.

That means encouragement, gratitude, hugs, kindness, shared laughter—those things matter. A lot. When we don't stay intentional about that, we slip. We start to focus on those things that irritate us. We criticize more than we celebrate. We get stuck in a loop of frustration, and it builds. That kind of cycle doesn't just create tension—it creates emotional distance. And over time, that distance turns into disconnection.

Gottman also identified four behaviors that signal a relationship is in real trouble: criticism, defensiveness, contempt, and stonewalling. When you live in a place where you're constantly picking each other apart, you invite those very things into the relationship—sometimes without even realizing it.

Here's the good news: you can change that behavior. You can choose to water the flowers instead of focusing on the weeds.

We invite you to pause and look for the good. You can choose to notice the effort, the character, the little things that show love in quiet ways. Because whatever you choose to notice is what you will see.

What we feed will grow

The idea is simple: what you "feed" will grow. You will get more of what you focus on, for better or worse. If you choose to focus on the positive qualities, the strengths, and the actions that you admire in your partner, child, neighbor, colleague, or whomever you want to deepen your connections with, you will see these qualities flourish. **Positive reinforcement** doesn't just improve the relationship, it strengthens it. By **actively appreciating and complimenting** the good traits you see in others, you nurture the connection.

Studies in **positive psychology**, particularly the work of Dr. Martin Seligman, emphasize the importance of focusing on **strengths** instead of weaknesses. This approach doesn't ignore flaws but encourages us to highlight and appreciate the positive aspects of others, making us more resilient as a couple or in any relationship. When you focus on strengths, it activates positive emotions, increases trust, and builds a stronger foundation for the relationship.

For example, expressing appreciation for someone's hard work, kindness, or intelligence can foster greater feelings of **emotional**

security and **self-esteem**. In fact, a study from the *University of California, Berkeley* found that couples who regularly express **gratitude** for each other experience higher levels of relationship satisfaction and intimacy. By giving compliments and offering genuine praise, you reinforce positive behaviors, which encourages them to flourish.

The role of criticism and how to avoid It

Criticism is the invasive, noxious weed that kills the lawn. It's a habit that is easy to fall into, especially when you feel frustrated or disappointed. Just like weeds, criticism has a **detrimental impact** on the health of the relationship. **Constant negative feedback** can trigger the **fight-or-flight response**, increasing stress levels and emotional tension. Over time, this will lead to a breakdown in communication and connection.

Instead, when you choose to provide constructive, authentic feedback tactfully and kindly, you ensure that the relationship stays **emotionally safe**. According to Dr. Sue Johnson, a leading expert in relationship therapy, emotional safety is crucial for deepening intimacy and connection. When individuals feel emotionally safe, they are more likely to engage in **vulnerable conversations**, leading to greater understanding and connection.

Practical ways to water the flowers

So, how does a person water the flowers? It starts with being intentional and mindful in how you interact with those you care about. Here are some practical ways to do this:

1. **Express appreciation regularly.** Acknowledge a person's efforts, whether they're big or small. Try saying, "I appreciate how thoughtful you were today" or "You did such a great job handling that situation." This reinforces the good qualities and encourages them to continue.

2. **Give compliments.** Genuine compliments go a long way. They make a person feel good, and they also help build a positive environment in the relationship. Complimenting their kindness,

skills, or sense of humor reminds them of the qualities that make them special and provide the fertile ground for the flowers to grow.

3. **Practice gratitude.** Start each day by reflecting on what you're grateful for in your partner or friends or colleagues. Share your appreciation openly, whether it's for their support, their patience, or just the fact that they support you.

4. **Focus on what they do well:** Instead of pointing out mistakes or flaws, highlight the strengths and efforts your partner is making. This positive feedback encourages a growth mindset, where both of you feel supported in developing together.

5. **Communicate positively:** Focus on using "I" statements to express how you feel, rather than blaming or accusing. For instance, instead of saying, "You never listen to me," try, "I feel unheard when we don't have honest discussions."

The science behind focusing on the positive

Research from the *Harvard Study of Adult Development* has shown that strong, supportive relationships are a key predictor of long-term happiness and life satisfaction. People who experience positive, nurturing relationships report better physical health, greater life satisfaction, and lower levels of stress. Relationships that thrive on positivity and appreciation lead to **deeper emotional bonds** and more fulfilling lives.

When people focus on the positive, their brains release **dopamine** and **oxytocin**, the chemicals associated with happiness and bonding. This not only improves their emotional well-being but also strengthens the connection they have with others.

By shifting your focus from the weeds to the flowers, you make the conscious choice to nurture and grow your relationships. Just like watering grass, when you give your relationships the attention, positivity, and care they need, they'll thrive and flourish into something even more beautiful. Feed what you want to grow, and watch your connections deepen, strengthen, and bloom.

Chapter 11 Reflection Questions

1. When you think about the relationships you value most, what are the "flowers" you see—those qualities, moments, or traits that make you appreciate this person?

2. What "weeds" have you been focusing on lately? How has that focus affected how you feel toward this person?

Which of the four Gottman "relationship killers" (criticism, defensiveness, contempt, stonewalling) have you noticed creeping into your relationships—either from you or toward you?

Chapter 11 Challenge

Challenge 1: Five-to-One in Action

For the next week, consciously aim for *five positive interactions* for every one negative interaction with someone important to you. This could be compliments, hugs, sending a funny meme, or doing a thoughtful gesture. Track it each day and notice the difference in the tone of your relationship.

Challenge 2: Weed-to-Flower Shift

Pick one "weed" you've been focusing on in a relationship. For the next seven days, when you catch yourself noticing it, intentionally shift your focus to one "flower" instead. Write down the flowers you notice so you can see them multiplying.

Challenge 3: The Gratitude Text

Send one short but specific text each day this week to a friend, partner, or family member expressing something you appreciate about them. It doesn't have to be deep—sometimes "Thanks for always making me laugh" is enough to water a flower.

Challenge 4: Compliment Out Loud

The next time you *think* something positive about someone, say it out loud instead of keeping it in your head. This can be with anyone—your spouse, your child, a coworker, or a friend at school pickup.

Challenge 5: Humor Break

At least once this week, choose to replace criticism with humor. Instead of pointing out that the dishwasher is loaded "wrong," make a lighthearted joke or simply say "Thanks for helping" and let it go.

Chapter 12:
Conclusion

In the end, connection isn't found, it's cultivated. We don't stumble into closeness by accident. We build it bit by bit through attention, compassion, and care. Like any garden, the relationships we treasure need the most attention. Relationships need to be noticed, nourished, and given room to grow.

You've now read the stories, been introduced to the tools, and discovered the truths about what it means to connect with curiosity, imagination, presence, and purpose. But none of it matters if we don't water what matters most.

The relationships in your life don't need to be perfect. They need to be real. They need you—your time, your words, your willingness to see the good and call it out loud. Don't wait for the other person in the relationship to make the first move. Be the one who waters the flowers.

And when it feels hard—because it will—remember this: love grows where effort lives. Joy blooms where gratitude is spoken. Healing happens where kindness is consistent.

So, choose to notice. Choose to nurture. Choose to water the flowers. Take 100% responsibility for the relationships and connections in your life.

Because that's how connections are kept; that's how love stays alive.

One of the families in Richard's neighborhood had raised and cared for a beautiful daughter who had severe disabilities that kept her in a wheelchair and bedbound her entire life. Her inability to feed and care for herself meant her mother lived her life in 2-hour cycles: her other activities had to revolve around a 12 times-a-day/365 days-a-year feeding, bathing, and other care schedule. When this child was born the father built a career around the need to provide healthcare for this tender soul. This couple raised other children and have always been active, caring, and supportive neighbors but their level of interaction with the neighborhood has always, appropriately and necessarily, revolved around caring for their daughter.

Not long ago, at the age of 27, their daughter passed away. It has been hard on all of them, especially her mother who felt the pain acutely. For over 27 years this mother's life had literally revolved around the life-preserving needs of her child.

In a similar vein, a few weeks ago, Christine got a call late at night. She almost didn't answer (assuming it was a "butt dial")—she was exhausted, had an early morning, and figured it could likely wait. But she picked up. The voice on the other end cracked: "I didn't know who else to call."

That moment reminded her of this truth: connection doesn't always come when it's convenient—but when it's *needed*. And sometimes, just showing up—just answering—is everything.

When we take time to ponder all of our interactions, we may feel that we are only making a difference based on the volume of the connections we make.

In a world influenced by social media, it's common for people to claim they have scores, hundreds, thousands, or millions of "friends" and "followers." Whether the claims are accurate or not, it creates a feeling that we need a lot of connections to have value. Yet, as in the cases of Richard's neighbor or Christine's friend, we have come to discover that it's those who truly need us that create the connections that matter most.

And that's how we grow something beautiful: together.

–Christine and Richard

About the Authors

Richard Godfrey - Co-Founder & CEO, Avec-me (WITH me)

Richard Godfrey is the Co-Founder and CEO of Avec-me (WITH me), a consultancy dedicated to helping individuals, leaders, and teams build stronger connections that fuel positive energy, drive results, and reduce conflict.

With more than 40 years in leadership and personal development, Richard has coached Fortune 100 CEOs, senior military commanders, government leaders, and frontline teams across industries including automotive, finance, healthcare, aviation, and public administration.

The author of nine books on the link between relationship strength and performance, Richard has also co-authored and ghostwritten international bestsellers with Wall Street Journal, New York Times, Amazon, and Times of London award-winning authors. He has collaborated with leadership icons such as Dr. Stephen R. Covey, Stephen M.R. Covey, Ken Blanchard, and Hyrum W. Smith, and developed over two dozen training programs for organizations including the U.S. Marine Corps, General Motors, UnitedHealthcare, Bank of America, and the Governments of Canada and Saudi Arabia.

Richard and his wife, Heather, live in Utah and cherish their nearly 45 years of marriage, two children, and beloved granddaughter.

Christine Lavulo, CPSC – Co-Founder and CEO of RelierWITH and ConnexionsLab

Christine is a Best-Selling Author, Certified Professional Success Coach, Canfield Success Principles Trainer and Maxwell Leadership Speaker, Coach and Trainer. She is the Co-Founder and CEO of RelierWITH and ConnexionsLab, where she focuses on using all her various tools and experiences to help individuals and organizations connect deeper and have more successful relationships – both personal and professional.

Christine has had a successful corporate career working with companies like FranklinCovey, Center of Excellence for Higher Education, and Deseret Digital Media. But her entrepreneurial spirit also led her to pursue her own business when she became a licensed Realtor in 2002. Her focus was to assist first time home buyers in achieving the "American Dream". In addition, she ran a successful home staging company.

Christine has served on various boards including the Salt Lake Executive Association, the West High Alumni Association, as well as serving as the first President for the Salt Lake Chapter of the International Association of Home Staging Professionals (IAHSP), and Director of Mentees for Women of Worth (WOW), and Fast Pitch Director for LDSPMA. She currently serves as an Advisory Board member for Promise 2 Live.

Christine and her husband, Clawson, live in North Salt Lake, UT and have 5 sons, 3 daughter-in-laws and 5 grandchildren. Those connections are truly what matter most.

Ready to Keep Building Deeper Connections?

The journey doesn't end here—it begins WITH you.

You've just discovered tools that can transform the way you connect—with your partner, your family, your friends, and even your team at work.

Now it's time to put those insights into action and keep growing alongside others who are committed to doing the same.

At **www.connexionslab.com**, you'll find resources created to help you *live* what you've learned in *Connect Deeper*.

- **Free Resources & Reflection Guides** to strengthen your relationships every day

- **The Connect Deeper Course** – a self-paced online experience to help you practice the 5 Questions in real life

- **Group Coaching with Christine Lavulo** – join others on an 8-week guided journey toward lasting connection

- **Workshops & Trainings** – for individuals, couples, and organizations ready to create "WITH Spaces" and lead through connection

Continue your journey. Deepen your relationships. Live *WITH* intention.

Visit **www.Connect-Deeper.com** to explore all the ways you can **Connect Deeper** today.

References

Abrams, Z. (2023, June 1). The Science of Why Friendships Keep us Healthy. *Monitor on Psychology, 54*(4). https://www.apa.org/monitor/2023/06/cover-story-science-friendship

Johnson, M. H., Griffin, R., Csibra, G., Halit, H., Farroni, T., de Haan, M., Tucker, L. A., Baron-Cohen, S., & Richards, J. (2005). The Emergence of the Social Brain Network: Evidence From Typical and Atypical Development. *Development and Psychopathology, 17*(3), 599–619. https://doi.org/10.1017/S0954579405050297

Tupes, E. C., & Christal, R. E. (1992). Recurrent personality Factors Based on Trait Ratings. *Journal of Personality, 60*(2), 225–251. https://doi.org/10.1111/j.1467-6494.1992.tb00973.x

www.ingramcontent.com/pod-product-compliance
Lightning Source LLC
Chambersburg PA
CBHW070116080526
44586CB00013B/1312